D0636627

Columbia University

Contributions to Education

Teachers College Series

No. 834

AMS PRESS
NEW YORK

Methods of Lesson Observing

by

Preservice Student-Teachers

A Comparative Study

by

ROLAND HENRY CHATTERTON, Ph.D.

TEACHERS COLLEGE, COLUMBIA UNIVERSITY
CONTRIBUTIONS TO EDUCATION, NO. 834

BUREAU OF PUBLICATIONS
Teachers College · Columbia University
NEW YORK · 1941

Library of Congress Cataloging in Publication Data

Chatterton, Roland Henry, 1901-
    Methods of lesson observing by preservice student-
teachers.

    Reprint of the 1941 ed., issued in series: Teachers
College, Columbia University. Contributions to educa-
tion, no. 834.
    Originally presented as the author's thesis, Columbia.
    Bibliography: p.
    1. Observation (Educational method). I. Title.
II. Series: Columbia University. Teachers College.
Contributions to education, no. 834.
LB1731.C44   1972   370'.733   72-178801
ISBN 0-404-55834-8

Reprinted by Special Arrangement with Teachers
College Press, New York, New York

From the edition of 1941, New York
First AMS edition published in 1972
Manufactured in the United States

AMS PRESS, INC.
NEW YORK, N. Y.   10003

ACKNOWLEDGMENTS

For assistance in the development of this study, the writer acknowledges special indebtedness to the members of his dissertation committee: Professor Florence B. Stratemeyer, sponsor, Professor Helen M. Walker, and Professor Edward S. Evenden.

He wishes particularly to express appreciation to his wife, Emma Gosman Chatterton, whose unfailing encouragement and practical assistance have helped immeasurably to make possible this study. For cooperation in conducting the experiment, he is also grateful to the members of the class of 1939 at Rhode Island College of Education who were the observers; to Professors Marion D. Weston, Eugene Tuttle, Amy A. Thompson, and Wendela C. Carlson, who, as members of the college faculty, assisted in the capacity of judges during the observations; to Misses Lina F. Bates, Isabel M. Woodmancy, Marjorie L. Bean, and Helen M. Triggs, who, as teachers, conducted the observed classes in the demonstration school of the college; and to the supervisors of training, who, while enrolled in the 1936 course designated as ss228MG in Teachers College, Columbia University, assisted in the refinement of A Check List for the Observation of Pupil Activities in the Classroom.

Acknowledgment is also made for the gracious permission of the following publishers to reprint excerpts from their books: Collegiate Press, Inc., Ames, Iowa; Bureau of Publications, Teachers College, Columbia University; World Book Company, Yonkers-on-Hudson, New York; Public School Publishing Co., Bloomington, Illinois; United States Bureau of Education, Government Printing Office, Washington, D. C.; and Yale University Press, New Haven, Connecticut.

R. H. C.

CONTENTS

CHAPTER   PAGE

I. DESCRIPTION OF STUDY AND OF OBSERVATION AS A PART OF
   TEACHER-EDUCATION   1
   Preview of the Study   1
       Statement of the Study   1
       Observers and Observees   1
       Subjects Were Groups of Observers   1
       Use of Check List as Measurement of Observation .   2
   Present Status of Observation in Teacher-Education .   2
       Terminology   2
       Extent of Observation in Teacher-Education . .   3
   Necessary Arrangements for the Study   6
       Appropriate Observational Facilities   6
       Preliminary Preparation of Observers   6
       Observational Techniques Investigated   6

II. DEVELOPMENT OF PROCEDURES FOR OBSERVATIONAL STUD-
    IES IN EDUCATION   8
    Establishment of Scientific Observation   8
        Free and Directed Observation   8
        Early Trend toward Scientific Observation . . . 8
        Review of Literature, and Explanation of Its Pres-
            entation in This Chapter   9
        Basic Studies That Used Observational Procedures   10
        Some Child Development Monographs   13
        Fundamental Controls for Observational Research   16
    Use of the Observational Method in Six Types of
        Studies   19
        Social Behavior and Adjustment of Nursery School
            Children   19
        Preschool Children's Responses to Psychological
            Tests   20
        Normative Studies of Children's Developmental
            Behavior   21
        Children's Extrovert Behavior   21

CHAPTER   PAGE

Study of Child Personality in Classroom Situation .   22
Simultaneous Observation of All Pupils in Class-
room Situation   23
Comparison of the Writer's Study with the Foregoing
Types of Studies   24
Observers as Subjects of Experiment   24
Large Number of Observers   24
A Group Experiment   25
Similar Controls   25
Comparison with Studies of Classroom Situations .   25
Measurement of Observation   25

III. PREVALENT TECHNIQUES OF CLASSROOM OBSERVATION AND
THEIR MEASUREMENT BY MEANS OF A CHECK LIST . .   26
Investigation of Classroom Observational Techniques   26
Description of the Code Used in This Study . . .   28
Development of a Check List for Measuring Classroom
Observation   29
A Check List for the Observation of Pupil Activities
in the Classroom   32

IV. DESCRIPTIVE ACCOUNT OF EXPERIMENTAL ARRANGEMENTS
AND PROCEDURE   38
Grouping of Observers   38
Observees   39
Judges   39
Observation of Ten Lessons   40
Directions Given to Observers   41
At Time of Check Lists' Distribution One Week
Prior to First Preliminary Observation . . .   41
Prior to First Preliminary Observation   46
Prior to Second Preliminary Observation . . .   47
Prior to Third Preliminary Observation   49
Prior to First of Ten Experimental Observations .   49
Reliability of the Method   51

V. STATISTICAL TREATMENT OF DATA   52
Method of Comparing Groups of Observers . . .   52
Comparison of Four Groups, Each Using Different Ob-
servational Technique   53
Comparison of Code Groups with Non-Code Groups .   56

CHAPTER   PAGE

Comparison of Groups on the Basis of Amount of Pu-
pil Participation Categories and Type of Pupil Ac-
tivity Categories   57
Comparison of Code Group with Code Plus Teacher's
Objective Group   60
Agreement of Judges   60

VI. LIMITATIONS OF THE STUDY   64
Arrangement of the Experiment as a Comparative
Study of Groups of Observers   64
Limitations of the Check List's Use   64
Fundamentals for Providing Observation in Keeping
with Recognized Educational Theory   66
Compromise between Theory and Practice in Observa-
tion   69

VII. SUMMARY AND CONCLUSIONS   71

CLASSIFIED BIBLIOGRAPHY   74

APPENDIX

A. Teachers' Objectives for the Ten Observed Lessons . .   83
B. Stenographic Reports of the Ten Observed Lessons . .   88
C. General Matters Pertaining to Observation   136

TABLES

TABLE   PAGE

1. Prevalence of Observational Techniques Used in Representative Teachers Colleges 26

2. Prevalence of Observational Guide Sheets Used in Representative Teachers Colleges 28

3. Mean Score and Standard Deviation for Four Observational Groups Equated According to Scores on the Check List 38

4. Analysis of Variance of Mean Scores of Individual Students for Four Groups Using Different Observational Techniques 53

5. Mean Scores, Mean Squares, and F Values for the Analysis of Variance References of This Chapter ....:.............. 54

6. Analysis of Variance of Mean Scores of Individual Students for Combined Code Groups and Combined Non-Code Groups 57

7. Analysis of Variance of Mean Scores of Individual Students in Pupil Participation Categories for Combined Code Groups and Combined Non-Code Groups 58

8. Analysis of Variance of Mean Scores of Individual Students in Type of Pupil Activity Categories for Combined Code Groups and Combined Non-Code Groups 58

9. Results of Analysis of Variance of Mean Scores of Individual Students in Pupil Participation Categories, Comparing Group I with Each of the Other Three Groups 59

10. Number of Judges Agreeing in the Marking of Categories in Each of the Ten Lessons 61

CHAPTER I

Description of Study and of Observation as a Part of Teacher-Education

PREVIEW OF THE STUDY

Statement of the study. It is the custom in institutions specializing in the preparation of teachers to provide for practice in the observation of classroom activities. Few investigations have been made of this phase of teacher-preparation, as will be shown later in this chapter. However, numerous studies using the observational method have been made in fields other than that of teacher-training, and many of the procedures and controls developed in these studies may now be applied to the student-teacher's observation of class activities. By means of these developments, it is the purpose of this study to compare common observational techniques used by student-teachers when observing classes of pupils.

Observers and observees. One hundred and thirty-six student-teachers were the observers of ten classroom lessons in arithmetic, English, and social studies presented in rotation. The observees consisted of four groups of twenty-four pupils each. These pupils were enrolled in the campus demonstration school of a teachers college. The children and their teachers were thoroughly accustomed to carrying on their classroom activities in the presence of visitors and classes of observers.

Subjects were groups of observers. The subjects of this experiment were the one hundred thirty-six observers, who were divided into four equated groups of thirty-four members each. Their observations provided the group-data for this comparative study. Each group used a different observational technique. The four groups observed simultaneously the same lessons, and each group retained the same observational technique throughout the experiment. The four techniques were:

1. Recording full running notes.
2. Making no record or notations.
3. Using five codes, symbolical of the manner in which pupils participated.
4. Using the same codes and receiving, prior to each lesson, a statement of the teacher's major objective.

Use of check list as measurement of observation. After lessons were observed by the four observational techniques listed above, the observers interpreted their records on a specially prepared form that was used by all groups. This form, called a check list, contained lists of multiple-choice items that described various class situations. Details of the experimental set-up and procedure are explained in Chapters III and IV.

The need for studies in observation will be made clear in the following sections on the place and extent of observation in teacher-training curricula.

PRESENT STATUS OF OBSERVATION IN TEACHER-EDUCATION

Terminology. The place of classroom observation in the preparation of teachers can be shown by stating its relationship to student-teaching, and by indicating some pertinent issues involved in current practices. Although many investigations have been made in the student-teaching phase of teacher-education, comparatively few have pertained to this more restricted phase, namely, the student-teacher's observation of pupils' classroom activities. The association of observation with student-teaching has been clearly stated by Marshall [5 : 1932]:*

Student-teaching . . . includes all the activities in which the student-teacher engages while working in the training school . . . student activi-

* Throughout this study, each source of information is indicated by two numbers in brackets. The first refers to the number of the reference to be found in the Bibliography; the second refers to the publication date of the reference.

ties are defined as activities relating to the observation of teaching, activities relating to assisting the room teacher or critic (participation), and activities relating to teaching and including actual teaching. These three —observation, participation, and responsible teaching—comprise student-teaching and are broad enough to include most of the activities of the student-teacher.

This quotation suggests that observation is an essential part of an effective teacher-training program. We may now look to other studies to determine the extent and variation of current practices.

Extent of observation in teacher-education. A questionnaire by Williams [7 : 1922] obtained data showing that observation was being done in 234 out of 295 institutions replying, including normal schools, colleges, and universities that offered educational courses. In about two-thirds of these it was found that observation was combined with one or more other courses and that there seemed to be an increasing tendency to follow this practice.

Facts regarding the provision of observation and its relation to other courses were similarly revealed in the more inclusive study, *The National Survey of the Education of Teachers* [6 : 1933]. This study showed that almost nine-tenths of the investigated teacher-training institutions offered work in observation, and that there was a distinct tendency for the normal schools and teachers colleges to connect this work with other courses, "the ratio being about three combining it with other courses to two that offered it separately."

These surveys reveal a decided tendency toward applied observational procedures in teacher-training institutions. In the investigation conducted by the writer, the student-observers had had weekly periods of observation extending over a year and a half and these periods were connected with courses in educational psychology and in principles of teaching. The students made no written records during these observations. Immediately following each observed lesson there was a discussion under the leadership of the college professor and the demonstration teacher.

At Rhode Island College of Education, where this experiment was conducted, the plan of arranging for observations enables the college students to be introduced to the various activities of the classroom in their freshman year. This is accomplished through a system of rotating small groups of students so that they may observe classes at the several levels or grades of instruction during some part of the year. Members of the college faculty and teachers of the demonstration school cooperate to make meaningful this initial experience of the student-observers. In the sophomore year, all students attend weekly demonstrations of the various classroom lessons that are current in a modern school. Regular teachers in the demonstration school conduct these lessons with the pupils that are enrolled in their classrooms.

Armentrout [1 : 1924] has mentioned the desirability of early observation as practiced at Colorado State Teachers College:

> It is generally agreed that the student's active contact with the training school should not be limited to the actual period of student-teaching. As soon as possible after the student enters the college, he should be introduced to actual problems of teaching through directed observation.

Another plan of meeting the issue of early association between the student's college instruction and his contacts with the demonstration school is in use at Montclair State Teachers College in New Jersey. Here members of the college faculty do the teaching in the campus demonstration school. This arrangement affords the college students ample opportunities to associate their instruction with observation of educational theories as they are applied in practice by their professors.

According to Henderson's [4 : 1937] investigation of student-teaching in state teachers colleges, plans of cooperation between the college and its demonstration school, such as those mentioned above, are uncommon. In his summary he shows the wide variation in the types of observation available. To quote:

> Very few of the colleges had observations for students organized or conducted in accordance with professional opinion on the subject. The students were not required to do enough observational work, and the observations they did make were not organized for definite purposes.

Wide variation in the manner in which observation is conducted in student-teaching courses designed for the training of secondary teachers is indicated in a study by Flowers [3 : 1932]. This study revealed that in connection with subject-matter courses, students observed class work for specific teaching techniques and procedures in 39 out of 54 institutions considered. In connection with professional or theory courses, students observed class work for specific teaching techniques and procedures in 44 out of 50 institutions considered. The median number of hours of the student-teaching course devoted to observation was 25 and the median number of hours devoted to actual teaching was 72. Interpreted by percentages, the median number of hours in observation was 15 per cent of the total time, but for the individual institutions the range was from 2.5 per cent to 50 per cent.

In the sixth volume of the *National Survey of the Education of Teachers,* Evenden [2 : 1933] summarizes and interprets many of these diversified practices of teacher-training institutions in regard to their arrangements for observation, participation, and practice-teaching. The summary pertaining to observation shows that the "observation of teaching is spread over the entire length of the curriculum by some, and concentrated in a two or three point separately organized course by others."

The foregoing reviews disclose that observation has an important place in teacher-training curricula but that its amount and arrangement differ according to the institution. Other issues that must be carefully considered before undertaking an experiment dealing with groups of observers are the appropriateness of the facilities and the preparation of the observers.

NECESSARY ARRANGEMENTS FOR THE STUDY

Appropriate observational facilities. This experiment was conducted in a specially designed demonstration room which has adequate facilities for a large group of students to observe a class of pupils. The room permits the observers to be seated in a balcony with rows of seats sloping upward and backward around the sides and back of a classroom. The first row of observers in the balcony is seated about five feet above the floor of the classroom. Two additional rows of observers are elevated in usual balcony manner. These three balcony-rows accommodate one hundred and forty-five observers. Under such conditions student-observers have unobstructed view of all activities that are being conducted by the pupils in the demonstration room. Details regarding seating of the observers during the experiment are given in Chapter IV.

Preliminary preparation of observers. Both in the theory courses including educational psychology and principles of teaching and in the previous half year of observations, emphasis had been placed upon the characteristics of scientific investigations, as summarized by Gates [75:1932]. This established the necessary understanding and attitudes for the students in their observational procedures.

The students had been further informed in these earlier observations how to observe without distracting the observees. Matters stressed included the necessity of refraining from any conversation, laughing, or other exclamations in response to pupils' activities, and being present before the start of the demonstration and remaining until pupils had left the demonstration room. The latter point was stressed for the additional purpose of insuring that the observers would be present for each full period of the demonstration so that they might be cognizant of the pupils' activities from the start of each lesson to its finish, and thus be able to comprehend the whole result.

Observational techniques investigated. Having briefly described the study and its connection with teacher-education, we come to the issue which relates to the main purpose of this study, namely, the comparative values of the observational techniques used by teachers-in-training. The problem of whether data concerning the activities of pupils in the classroom might best be secured by taking full running notes or by taking abbreviated notes in the form of commonly used codes with a seating chart, or by observing without any recording, is the major issue with which we are confronted in this experiment. The assistance derived from knowing the teacher's objective of the lesson prior to the observation is also investigated. With this issue in mind the next chapter will review the development of observational procedures and techniques. The fourth chapter will explain in detail the preparation of the observers for the experiment.

CHAPTER II

Development of Procedures for Observational Studies in Education

ESTABLISHMENT OF SCIENTIFIC OBSERVATION

Free and directed observation. Fundamentally, there are two types of observational methods—free or undirected observation and directed observation. In the first type the observer has no definite limitations to his observation. He may be intending to find or collect as much data as possible preliminary to further study. Although the use of free observation for making broad generalizations is not usually considered a scientific procedure, observations of this type often provide the basic facts that are necessary before scientific studies can be undertaken. In the directed type the observer follows defined objectives in making his observations. Frequently, he uses the facts gained from the free type to help in systematizing his directed observation.

Early trend toward scientific observation. It is interesting to note in the literature pertaining to the use of observational methods in education that slight evidences of scientific observation began to appear toward the close of the nineteenth century. An early article by Burnham [12 : 1891] contains the following quotation from the catalogue of Worcester State Normal School.

The principal requests the students to observe the conduct of children in all circumstances,—at home, at school, in the street, at work, at play, in conversation with one another and with adults,—and record what they see and hear as soon as circumstances will permit. When the nature of the work is explained to the school, great emphasis is placed upon the necessity of having the records genuine beyond all possibility of question; of having them consist of a simple concise statement of what the

8

child does or says, without comment by the writer; of making both the observation and the record without the knowledge of the child; and of noting the usual, rather than the unusual, conduct of the individuals observed. . . .

During this early transitional period, educators were becoming increasingly aware that their observational studies should be confined to restricted phases of the total environment, and that observers should make objective records without adding interpretations of them during the observational period.

Review of literature, and explanation of its presentation in this chapter. A few years ago certain basic studies prepared the way for the establishment of scientific procedures in observational research. Since then the authors of these and of many other investigations have continued to add to and adapt procedures with the result that there have been developed certain well established essentials which should be considered before conducting observational research. The presentation of this accumulating literature in the following pages will consist of three steps: first, describing the basic studies mentioned above; second, commenting upon some child development monographs showing the application of various observational techniques; and third, summarizing fundamental controls in procedures that these investigations reveal. Following this, additional studies using the observational method will be reviewed by dividing them into six types. The concluding section will compare these types of studies with the one by the writer. Studies to be reviewed generally used the observational method as a means toward an end, which was usually the investigation of personal traits or social reactions of individuals in their natural environment; they were not, as a rule, investigations of the observational method itself. It was to be expected that during the course of these various experiments, phases of the procedures were altered to meet the differing requirements of new observational studies and to make the investigations increasingly scientific. As a result many common elements and controls bearing upon all types and phases of observational techniques were made apparent.

Therefore, the following reviews will deal with the developments and use of these controls rather than with the findings related to the aims of the studies.

Basic studies that used observational procedures. Symonds [37 : 1926] made a close observational analysis of pupils' study habits at the secondary level. Behavior characteristics which revealed certain study habits and abilities of two groups of boys, alike in age and general ability, were noted. However, one of the groups was greatly superior in scholastic attainment. One boy at a time was observed in classrooms and study hall for the characteristics mentioned above. Complete notes were taken of thirty hours' observation of the study and recitation conduct of ten boys. The study stated that because of the insufficient number of pupils studied, it was inadvisable to consider the observations as demonstrative of real differences between the two groups. The study pointed the way toward future observational research in studying children.

Olson [33 : 1929] studied mannerisms, such as thumb-sucking, nail-biting, protruding of tongue, and pulling of hair, of individual children in elementary classrooms. In this investigation all pupils in a room were observed simultaneously. The technique provided for noting the occurrence of the children's mannerisms during consecutive short periods of time. The unit of measurement was one or more occurrences of the observed mannerism per period. For example, a child who did not bite his nails at any time during a five-minute period would score zero, while a child who bit his nails one or more times during the period would score only one for that period. If there were twenty periods it would be possible to score twenty. A chart of the pupils' seating arrangements in the room was used and the records of the various pupils were entered directly in their respective spaces on this chart. The introduction of this method made possible quantitative analysis of data concerning the behavior characteristics of groups of pupils under normal conditions.

Olson's procedure, known as the method of short samples, provided for the observation of the ordinary activities of observees for definite periods of time. The number and length of the periods were the same for all observed individuals in order to make quantitative treatment of the data possible. Also the individuals were observed under similar conditions. An article by Goodenough [17:1928] presented a complete descriptive summary of this observational method. Goodenough and Anderson [18:1931] concluded that a particular advantage of this method was its economy of time; the technique allowed a group of pupils to be observed simultaneously in approximately the amount of time required for the individual method. They mentioned as defects of the method that it was not well suited to more complicated behavior; and that when all observations were made in sequence, unusual conditions affecting the subjects at the particular time of the observation might cause unnatural behavior to be recorded.

A different observational technique for studying child personality at the kindergarten level was used by Rugg, Krueger, and Sondergaard [35:1929]. This technique, known as the technique of the eye-witness analyst, provided a complete running account of the succession of experiences through which child personality develops. Each of twenty-seven children was observed for three fifteen-minute periods. A highly skilled observer having stenographic assistance recorded everything the child said or did, and everything said by the children with whom the observed child was closely associated. The analysis of the language records revealed the predominant traits of the kindergarten children.

An early volume by Thomas and Associates [38:1929] discussed techniques for studying social behavior. The studies described were pioneer contributions in the field of experimental sociology. Their purpose was to find means of recording factors in the natural environment which affected an individual's overt behavior. These records were then to be used to determine the consistency of an individual's behavior over a period of time and to detect variations among individuals. The method of short samples was used to provide quantitative units which would measure overt activities. A major conclusion of these studies was that the study of social behavior could best be made by measuring individual's overt actions that involved other persons, materials, and self.

The measurement of contacts with other people and with material has been amplified in later observational studies of behavior patterns by Thomas and Others [39 : 1933]. By means of the method of short samples observations were made of social-behavior patterns in such groups as nursery school, kindergarten, trade school, and adult industrial work. These behavior patterns consisted of three categories showing self-activity, activities involving contacts with other persons, and activities involving contacts with things. Data were recorded by means of codes representing many different items under each category. Examples of these codes are shown below:

Self-activity patterns
N_1—Daydreaming.
N_2—Talking to self, singing and vocalizing.
and so forth.

Social activity patterns
S_1—Observation of persons.
S_2—Approach to persons.
and so forth.

Material activity patterns
M_1—Observation of material alone.
M_2—Approach to materials alone.
and so forth.

By analyzing such records of the observed individuals and the records of the sampling periods for each of the categories of behavior patterns, data were obtained for quantitative treatment. There appeared to be a problem in using such coded records during the sampling periods because of the differing interpretations that might arise in observing behavior patterns. In addition to the quantitative data recorded by codes, the observers made descriptive notes of the children's contacts regarding the initiator of the contacts and the recipient of the contacts. These notes made the quantitative data more meaningful.

Careful attention was given not only to the form of records but to the choice and preparation of observers as well. The necessity for this, as indicated by the volume's emphasis upon the use of the natural, social environment, required the experimental controls to be more concerned with the observer than with the situation. Nine essentials in the ability, capacity, and training of observers have been reviewed by Symonds [81 : 1931].

These few basic studies illustrate the beginning of systematic procedures in the observational method. These procedures were recognized as distinct contributions to research because they allowed direct quantitative and qualitative study of the behavior of individuals with little interference with their normal, social environments. The studies also brought out evidences of types of activities and behavior contacts that could best be studied by this method.

Some Child Development Monographs. The volume by Thomas and Associates [38 : 1929] was the beginning of a series of investigations concerning the behavior of preschool children that has been termed *Child Development Monographs*. These investigations were conducted for the most part in connection with nursery schools of the Child Development Institute of Teachers College, Columbia University. One of their main purposes was to further the development of techniques that would yield improved data concerning specific types of social behavior. In order to study certain specific phases of behavior patterns involving persons, material, and self, the first few monographs of the series continued to investigate the techniques used in Thomas' monograph.

Some of the later monographs delimited the scope of these first studies and further refined the observational technique. A single aspect of the social behavior of nursery school children, namely, physical contact, was investigated by Loomis [24 : 1931]. In order to reveal characteristic individual differences the specific objective was the development of a technique for the systematic exploration of the physical contacts made spontaneously by preschool children. Thirty-seven preschool children were the subjects of the investigation. Each child was observed in fifteen-minute periods during spontaneous activity when at least four other children were present. Descriptive notes as well as quantitative data were recorded. To help overcome errors in interpreting observations, category classifications were refined in the following manner:

Basis of Classification		*Category*
Role of person observed	(1)	Subject or initiator of contact
	(2)	Object or recipient of contact
Finer classification	(1)	Accident
of contact	(2)	Support
	(3)	Hit
	(4)	Push
	(5)	Pull
	(6)	Caress
	(7)	Exploration
	(8)	Assistance
	(9)	Pointing
Larger classification	(1)	Neutrality containing (1) and (2) of finer classifications
of contact	(2)	Aggression (3), (4), (5) above
	(3)	Cooperation (6), (7), (8), (9) above
Kind of response	(1)	Passivity
	(2)	Resistance
	(3)	Flight
	(4)	Cooperation

The study exercised considerable care to insure that the sampling of spontaneous behavior would be representative of the children's total physical contacts. The quantitative records were carefully analyzed to make certain that the situations involving equipment, adult relationships, and the like, did not favor any particular type of contact. Essential criteria of random sampling and illustrations of their violation in various types of studies have been considered by Walker [83 : 1929].

A monograph by Caille [13 : 1933] showed the use of three techniques to study the resistant behavior of preschool children. These were (1) the observation of preschool children,

(2) the analysis of stenographic reports of each child's language for two days, and (3) the analysis of his responses while taking intelligence tests. One thousand and two observational records of the children's behavior were made during their free play. Difficulties of two simultaneous observers in seeing the same reactions of the children were caused when:

(1) Someone stepped between observer and child observed just before the occurrence of the type of behavior being studied.

(2) Another child joined the group and the observers' eyes left the child observed in order to check the attendance of the newcomer.

(3) The two observers had an entirely different perspective because of their different positions in relation to the child.

(4) An observer was recording the details of one item of behavior when another occurred.

Thus we have a clear expression of four difficulties encountered by observers in obtaining objective observations. Other studies reviewed in this chapter show that efforts were made to control these difficulties by using an observers' balcony, by using a larger number of observers, or by following the observees more closely.

An investigation of the imaginative behavior of preschool children by means of observation during free play was reported in a monograph by Markey [26 : 1935]. Each of fifty-four children was observed during ten fifteen-minute periods which were distributed over a span of several months. Quantitative and qualitative data were obtained in regard to the frequency and the content of this type of behavior. The observations were rotated in order that all children would have similar lapses of time between observations. The hours of the observations were also rotated. In regard to the method of recording, certain controls of the observer were taken care of, such as the use of a special balcony for observers, the use of codes, and provision of a preliminary training period and practice. Many of these improved practices have been included in a laboratory manual by Wagoner [40 : 1935], which describes the preparation of observers and the procedures of observing young chil-

dren. These considerations have been more briefly summarized in a recent article by the same author [41 : 1937].

A study of preschool children's conflicts was reported in a
monograph by Jersild and Markey [23 : 1935]. It concerned the
aggressive, resistant, and hostile behavior of children between
two and four years of age. The investigation was one of nursery
school practices as well as psychology and sociology. The technique provided for an observer to follow a child and make
written records for periods of fifteen minutes at a time. Similar
and representative conditions were provided by spacing and
staggering observations of all children with respect to time of
day and day of week. Two observers made continuous written
records which showed in detail the physical activity of the
children, and additional notes recorded words spoken by them.
Each separate conflict or attack in which each child was involved, was identified according to specific categories during
the analysis of the data. Each of these was tallied under one
of four general headings, depending on what or whom the
overt acts of attack and defense centered, namely, (1) materials,
space, and activities; (2) the person of another . . . ; (3) verbal
acts . . . ; and (4) weeping, screaming, anger, and crying for
help. The study mentioned that the plan used raised the issues
of obtaining a true picture by the observer of conflict behavior
because of differing observer-interpretation, and of subse-
quently making a valid analysis of the items of activity that the
observer recorded. The study further revealed that discrepancies between two observers' accounts were largely caused by the
angle from which respective observers watched the behavior
and only partly by the matter of interpretation.

Before reviewing additional types of studies, we give below
a summary outline of the material presented up to this point in
the chapter. This outline indicates the controls that provide
for increasing precision in the observational method.

Fundamental controls for observational research. The
earliest systematic studies pertaining to the quantitative measurement of overt behavior had as their main goal the establishment of techniques that would give more satisfactory data

about the personal habits and social reactions of children. As a sequel to these studies, several investigators used and developed this new method of controlled observation. The following outline shows many of the observational controls which were used in the method's development.

A. Problems in sampling procedures:

    1. Distribution of time samples—

        The samples or periods of observation were distributed over longer periods of time in regard to time of day and day of week. This obviated the necessity of observing the children under possible abnormal, transitory conditions that might be present for a limited time.

    2. Representativeness of individual samples chosen for observation—

        Individual samples to be observed were chosen in such a manner that they were typical of the population concerning which the study's deductions were drawn.

    3. Rotation of observed individuals—

        Individual pupils to be observed were rotated in order that all children would have similar intervening lapses of time between observations.

    4. Adequacy of the number of observations—

        Generally, studies in observation were improved by increasing the number of samples. The number needed depended upon the frequency and variability of the occurrence of the behavior that was studied. Other associated factors included the accuracy with which the observational records were made, and the length of each time sample.

B. Problems in making records:

    1. Selection of recording phases of behavior—

        Since quantitative measures were desired, investigators selected factual aspects of behavior that could be most accurately observed and recorded. Examples of specific aspects: biting nails, physical contacts, and oral expressions (repeating words, crying, laughing, etc.) .

2. Wording of behavior categories (a category is a classification-group that comprises related discernible items)—

Records were taken from the normal social situations found in a classroom. These were items or units of behavior that could be recorded every time they occurred. The presence or absence of these behavior characteristics was numerically tabulated to constitute the units of measurement for the studies. The terminology of items was clearly defined in advance to assist observers in giving the same interpretations to the category. The wording of the categories and of their sub-classifications of items was arranged to make the meanings as mutually exclusive as possible.

3. Techniques of recording data—

Running notes and codes were generally used for collecting data. To prevent observers from being unable to record all necessary factors by code, descriptive notes accompanied the observations. In the studies where classes of pupils were observed, the codes of individual pupils' behavior were recorded on seating charts which showed each pupil's location in the classroom. Stenographic records were made of individual children's language. These were later analyzed according to predetermined categories.

C. Problems in observing behavior:

1. Position of observer in room—

Certain discrepancies in observation caused by the angle from which observers watched the behavior were overcome by having an observer on each side of the groups of which the observed individuals were a part, or by the use of a balcony overlooking the groups.

2. Practice and training of observer—

Provision was made for preliminary training and for practice by observers. Opportunities also were provided for memorizing the category-item meanings and the codes.

USE OF THE OBSERVATIONAL METHOD IN
SIX TYPES OF STUDIES

Social behavior and adjustment of nursery school children.
Several studies using the short sampling technique have been
concerned with the effect of nursery school attendance upon
the behavior of preschool children. In most cases the children's
behavior was observed during play activities. The study by
Jersild and Fite [22 : 1937] had a twofold purpose: to discover
quantitative trends in the effect of nursery school experience
on children's social behavior, and to appraise the social adjust·
ments of individual children. The procedure was mainly that
of direct observation by means of running diary accounts of
two groups of children—one with and one without previous
nursery school experience. Case records of individual children
and reports by teachers were the additional data which were
used. Phases of the study dealt with group trends and individual characteristics concerning conflicts, leadership, imaginative behavior, resourcefulness, and the effect of nursery
school environment. Independent records of simultaneous
observers, when compared item by item, showed high agreement. By collecting data from a variety of sources undue de-
pendence was not placed upon numerical data without description. This caution recognized that although two children
might have practically the same scores on some phase of behavior, the two scores might mean quite different things. Mention was also made in the study of the "too favorable" procedure of noting simply the occurrence or non-occurrence of
behavior without regard for its context.

Another investigation cautioning against too great de-
pendence upon one type of record was the investigation by
Murphy [30 : 1937], who made a psychological study of social
behavior and child personality with special attention to sympathetic behavior. In addition to codes and running notes an
inventory of behavior items and personality traits was taken
by means of a five-point scale to show the degree to which the
children exemplified the behavior.

A series of studies to determine the variation in children's behavior due to length of attendance in nursery school have shown a tendency to extend the length of the individual observational periods, and to extend the studies themselves over longer periods of time. Among these investigators are Ezekiel [15 : 1931], Parten [34 : 1932], Jack, Manwell, Mengert, and others [21 : 1934], Malloy [25 : 1935], and Hattwick [19 : 1936].

Similarities between the above studies and those previously mentioned under Child Development Monographs are apparent in that they make use of time sampling procedures and deal mainly with the behavior of preschool children. Children at this age lend themselves easily as subjects for the study of behavior and trait characteristics because they are sufficiently mature and yet not too molded to routine or adult organization. Examples of these sociological studies have been given here inasmuch as they constitute one of the most important types using the observational method.

Preschool children's responses to psychological tests. Observational studies have been made of children's responses during individual psychological examinations. Nelson [31 : 1931] investigated the total psychological test situation from the viewpoint of children's responses other than those called for by the test itself. The responses of each of one hundred and two three-year-old children were measured by checking items indicating sponstaneous activity, spontaneous conversation, initiative, and persistence. The test items that were resisted were also checked. Complete stenographic reports of the proceedings and conversation were recorded. From these records the responses other than intellectual were objectively measured and evaluated to determine the relation between them and intelligence. A closely allied study by Rust [36 : 1931] investigated a single phase of the above study, namely, the effect of resistance on intelligence test scores. Although these two studies are Child Development Monographs, they are included here because they illustrate a distinct type of study. In these studies children were observed with their examiner as individuals apart from their social groups.

Normative studies of children's developmental behavior.
Studies expressly devoted to the establishing of norms for
children's behavior have been made in the field of genetic
psychology. These are similar to investigations previously mentioned in that the observers systematically explored some particular sphere of young children's activity. The reports by
Bott and Bott [11 : 1928] on the observation of fundamental
habits in young children aimed at discovering problems arising out of fairly normal, routine situations. Evidences of the
most recurrent behavior patterns in children's play seemed to
be clearly indicated by three types of contacts, namely, materials, adults, and other children. Codes were used to record
these behavior patterns according to category-classifications.
Being a study in the interest of mental hygiene which seeks the
recognition of behavior deviations in order to institute pre-
ventive measures, it urged the establishment of a technique
for setting up norms of behavior.

Other studies in genetic psychology have been concerned
with the sequential nature of infants' developmental behavior.
Gesell and Thompson [16 : 1934] systematically observed one
hundred and seven infants at fifteen age levels from four to
fifty-six weeks. A specially enclosed crib having a one-way
vision screen was used. The examiner dictated complete accounts of his observations to a stenographer. In addition, cine-
matographic records were also made. By analyzing these accounts the infants' behavior was divided into seven categories.
Norms were found for initial evidences of various developments included under these categories.

The two studies mentioned above have been introduced not
because they contributed directly to the writer's study but
because they are examples of one of the important types of
educational studies showing the use of the observational
method to establish developmental norms.

Children's extrovert behavior. Newcomb [32: 1929] had
camp counselors make daily records of their observations of
certain traits noticed in fifty-one problem boys. These records
were used to study the consistency of certain intro-extrovert

behavior traits which had been chosen because of their mention by most writers on the subject. Greatest reliance was placed upon an observational study of children's extrovert behavior by Marston [27 : 1925]. Recorders were guided by the technique of choosing one of four statements to indicate the nature and degree of the boys' responses to each situation. In regard to the records, mention was made of the probability of error in recording selected responses rather than all possible sorts of them. This type of study exemplifies the use of the opinions of authorities as to the selection of traits to be observed. It is also somewhat unique in other respects, such as the free type of situation (camp) and use of atypical children (problem boys).

Study of child personality in classroom situation. The observation of individual personalities under classroom conditions presents still another type of study. Here, the specific behavior investigated usually consisted of activities, responses, or habits of pupils. Observational records of these were analyzed to provide greater understanding of differences among individuals. Remedial measures could then be instituted by teachers or others. Munkres [29 : 1934] made such a study by observing ten six-year-old children in a classroom situation. The problem was to discover children's patterns of behavior as revealed in the classroom, and to develop a check list that might help the teacher, or prospective teacher, to understand a child in reference to the situation in which he had his setting. To locate types of situations in which the child's behavior patterns were portrayed, three observers made fifteen simultaneous five-minute diary records of each child. Others interpreted the contents of each observer's diary and persons not familiar with the records matched them to detect similar behavior patterns. The content of these patterns upon which agreement was established formed the basis of the check list categories which covered such areas as social relationships, work relationships, position in group, emotional responses, and special manifestations. A limitation of the procedure mentioned by the study showed the difficulty of adequately determining the responses which entered into the making of personality estimates.

Eisner [14 : 1937] inquired into the value of an observational technique to be used by high school teachers, early in the term, to estimate their pupils' personalities as reflected in intelligence and industry. Such studies aimed at assisting the teacher to detect certain phases of pupils' personalities as they occurred in classroom settings.

Simultaneous observation of all pupils in classroom situation. The next two studies aimed at observing and recording simultaneously certain activities of all members of a class. Thus far, this had been done in but one of the studies reviewed in this chapter, namely, Olson's [33 : 1929]. Blume's [10 : 1929] study explained a technique to measure pupil attention. The measurement of both individual and group attention in the classroom was secured by making symbolic notations on a seating chart showing the respective locations of the individuals in the room. The seating chart technique had been developed by Dr. Leo J. Brueckner. The group attention-score, derived by recording and counting the periodic indications of pupils' attention in the room, was based on a method developed by Dr. Henry C. Morrison. Attention-profiles of individual pupils could be formulated from these scores. The study stated that the observer had to be prepared to note readily when the pupil was in attention. Other investigators have used similar techniques to determine the amount of responses, questions, and the like, by pupils in a classroom.

Controlled observational techniques for the purpose of obtaining objective measures of pupils' social performance factors in classrooms were investigated more recently by Wrightstone [43 : 1935]. Aspects of the educative process were grouped under the following defined categories of behavior: initiative, cooperation, consideration of others, enthusiasm, and memorization. A plan was devised to obtain a quantitative index of pupil participation in the activities included under each category by observing the frequency of their occurrence for specified units of time. These activities were recorded in code beside the appropriate pupils' names. A derived score controlling variables of time and number of pupils in the class was computed to permit records in different classes to be compared. A qualitative index was obtained from the observer's diary, in which pupils' expressions were analyzed on the basis of the category items. These accumulative notes were rated by several judges to indicate the degrees of quality of the different behavior-items. Another article by Wrightstone [42 : 1934] showed his development of a code-technique for evaluating certain aspects of group planning and discussion by pupils in the classroom.

This last type of study differed from others by using a technique which observed simultaneously all pupils of a classroom. The category classifications of things to observe were generally more pertinent to prevalent pupil activities in classrooms than to the personality of the individual. Various phases of pupil participation in the social activities of the classroom were especially included. The effectiveness with which socialized class procedures were being conducted in classrooms could be diagnosed by this technique.

COMPARISON OF THE WRITER'S STUDY WITH THE FOREGOING TYPES OF STUDIES

Although the comparison of four observational techniques used in appraising classroom lessons is a different type of study from any of the studies described, certain similarities as well as dissimilarities to these earlier studies can be recognized.

Observers as subjects of experiment. In the first place, most of the other studies were of social behavior per se, but this study used the observation of social behavior as the situation whereby a comparison of observational techniques used by teachers-in-training could be made. Stating this in terms of experimental subjects, others used observees as the subjects while here observers were the subjects.

Large number of observers. Being a group study of observational techniques rather than a study using observation solely as a technique of investigation, a large number of observers was required. In contrast to previously reviewed studies, where from one to three expert observers made simultaneous records, this study used four groups of thirty-four students each to make such records.

A group experiment. The formation of four groups of observers was possible because of the large number of subjects. It is with a study of this group behavior en masse rather than with the presence or extent of individual differences among observers that this experiment is concerned.

Similar controls. Controls similar to those used by other studies included the practice and training of observers and the use of a balcony for them. The observed situation was the same throughout the series of observations in regard to the number of pupils observed, the interval between school subject observations, the interval between pupil observations, the time of day, and the day of week.

Comparison with studies of classroom situations. Being a study concerned with the observational practice of teachers-in-training, the observers dealt with various activities of an entire class rather than with activities of one pupil at a time. In this respect the study is similar to Wrightstone's [43 : 1935] studies of pupil-activities relevant to initiative, cooperation, and the like. Other studies, such as Munkres [29 : 1934], dealt with the observation of individual personalities under classroom conditions. Naturally, since an individual, being observed in such a social situation, associated with various other individuals or small groups of them, the activities of these associates were included by Munkres to make the observed individual's record meaningful.

Measurement of observation. In order to measure the observation of certain activities of all pupils in the classroom, a check list of pupil activities was devised on the basis of the opinions of authorities on observational practices. As the marking of the check list was done by student-observers the agreement of expert judges was the criterion against which the students' observations were scored. The check list will be explained in detail in the next chapter.

CHAPTER III

Prevalent Techniques of Classroom Observation and Their Measurement by Means of a Check List

Investigation of classroom observational techniques. Prior to determining any values of observational techniques, the practices of representative teachers colleges in the United States were investigated to find the most frequently used techniques. This investigation was accomplished through the cooperation of forty-four supervisors of training who were enrolled in SS Education 228MG, Training School Problems, at Teachers College, Columbia University, and who represented teachers colleges and normal schools located in half the states of the Union. A questionnaire entitled General Matters Pertaining to Observation, which was filled out by each of the supervisors, is printed in Appendix C. The following table, Table 1, indicates the supervisors' responses in ranking the first, second, and third most prevalent observational techniques used in their localities.

Table 1

PREVALENCE OF OBSERVATIONAL TECHNIQUES USED IN REPRESENTATIVE TEACHERS COLLEGES

Technique	1st Rank	2d Rank	3d Rank
Running notes.........................	31	4	0
No record............................	7	9	2
Seating chart and code................	0	6	7
Any other technique..................	1*	0	0

* Uses form by Wrinkle and Armentrout [44:1932].

26

Table 1 shows that the *running notes* technique is most frequently used, the *no record* technique is the second most frequently used, and the *seating chart and code* technique is the third most frequently used. These are three of the techniques investigated by this study.

These three techniques may be clarified by brief descriptions. The writing of full *running notes* is used to record any overt behavior and oral expressions of the observees. The *no record* method avoids the recording of any data during the period of observation. In this case the observer devotes his entire attention to observing and makes no record of what he observes until the conclusion of the lesson. The third method of observing provides the observer with a class *seating chart* showing the room-locations of all the observees. The names of these observees are printed in their respective locations, which are designated by squares on the seating chart. Through the use of such a chart the observer can record pertinent information bearing upon his study by making notations within the proper squares. In order to facilitate this recording a code is constructed to represent the activities which the observer wishes to record.

The questionnaire further revealed that guide sheets are used in the majority of these teachers' colleges, and therefore the code technique plus the use of a prevalent type of guide sheet constitutes the fourth technique of observing. Guide sheets are used to provide student-observers with information regarding each lesson, or with what they are to look for in the lesson. To choose the type to be used in this study supervisors were asked to rank the first, second, and third most prevalent types of guide sheets used in their localities. Table 2 shows their responses.

Table 2 indicates that the most frequently used type of guide sheet shows the observer *what to look for in the lesson*. The second most frequently used type indicates the *major objective of the lesson*. Other procedures that are used provide reviews of the past work of the class, or copies of the teacher's lesson plan.

Table 2

PREVALENCE OF OBSERVATIONAL GUIDE SHEETS USED IN REPRESENTATIVE
TEACHERS COLLEGES

Guide Sheet Information	1st Rank	2d Rank	3d Rank
What to look for in lesson...............	15	7	2
Major objective of lesson................	7	9	1
Past work of class......................	5	0	6
Any other guide........................	2*	0	0
No guide sheet.........................	10	..	..

* Use teacher's lesson plan.

Although the guide sheet showing *what to look for in the lesson* ranked first, its purpose is fulfilled in this study by the use of a check list to be described later in this chapter. Therefore the type ranking second, *major objective of the lesson,* is chosen as the guide sheet to supplement the code in the fourth type known as *code plus teacher's objective* technique. The teachers' objectives for the ten observed lessons are included in Appendix A.

Description of the code used in this study. The code used in the third and fourth observational techniques was similar to the analysis card of pupil participation in the classroom which was devised by Raymond G. Drewry and Maxie N. Woodring and discussed by Mead [28:1930]. The five symbols that were chosen to represent the oral participation of the pupils were:

    a—answer, either voluntary or when called upon.
    v—voluntary contribution not directly called forth by a question.
    ?—questioned either the teacher or other pupils.
    r—report of individual or small group activity or of committee.
    p—play or printed material was read.

Other code outlines generally separated pupils' answers into *voluntary* and *called upon.* However, in practicing the use of a code preliminary to this study, the writer found it difficult to make this separation because pupils were frequently called upon from among several volunteers. Therefore, both kinds of answers to questions were coded by the same symbol, *a*. The new codes, *r* and *p*, were added in order to include practically every other possible situation of oral participation by pupils.

Development of a check list for measuring classroom observation. In order to have a uniform measuring instrument for all groups of observers, it was necessary to devise a list of observable classroom activities that were susceptible to categorical classification. A large number of observational manuals and outlines, prepared during recent years by supervisors of teacher-training for the purpose of aiding students to recognize various phases of classroom lessons, formed the basis of this list. The authors of these outlines included Armentrout [45 : 1927], Barr [46 : 1925], Blackhurst [47 : 1925], Brim [48], Brueckner [49 : 1930], Connor [50 : 1920], Daily [51 : 1932], Diemer and Melcher [52 : 1932], Fitzpatrick [53], Flowers [54 : 1926], Hopkins [55 : 1924], Jamaica Training School [56], Mead [57 : 1930], Michigan State Normal College [58 : 1923], Myers and Beechel [59 : 1926], Pryor [60 : 1931], Reeder and Reynolds [61 : 1931], Retan and Ross [62 : 1931], Russell [63 : 1924], Stratemeyer [64 : 1931], Department of Teachers Colleges and Normal Schools of Teachers College, Columbia University [65], [66], [67], University of Michigan, School of Education [68], and University of Texas, Department of Education [69].

During the analysis of the manuals different authors' suggestions, when similar, were listed together, and when dissimilar, formed the nuclei of new lists. Whenever three or more authorities agreed by having similar suggestions, these were incorporated in a final list of observable items, provided they indicated that the observational emphasis was upon pupil instead of teacher activity. This emphasis upon pupil activity was stressed because it is considered by many writers to be the best indication of the education taking place in the classroom. Supporters of this viewpoint pertaining to the measuring of teaching efficiency include Brueckner [70 : 1926], Collings [71 : 1926], Connor [72 : 1920], Herring [76 : 1924], Monroe and Clark [77 : 1924], Puckett [78 : 1928], Walker [84 : 1935], and Wrightstone [85 : 1934]. The observable items derived from the tabulated lists mentioned above were classified according to categories, each of which contained four or five of these items. In this manner a check list containing series of multiple-choice items was compiled for observers to use after they had concluded their observations of each lesson. It is evident that this check list provided the necessary guide sheet for directing the observers in what they were to look for in each of the lessons.

The forty-four supervisors, to whom reference was made previously in this chapter, refined the original phrasing of the category statements and their multiple-choice items by making observations in classrooms and using the check list as the observational guide sheet. Spaces under each item of the categories enabled the supervisors to write in their recommendations and their criticisms. Wherever more than one of the supervisors made the same criticism of an item, it was clarified accordingly.

A copy of the check list is presented herewith. It will be noticed that the total number of categories is twenty-five. Sixteen of these describe *types of pupil activity,* and nine indicate the *fraction of the class that participated* in types of pupil activity. The first categories are paired so that each category describing a type of pupil activity is followed by one that indicates the fraction of the class that participated in it. Directions to the observer preface the check list. An additional sheet that was issued to each observer explains the use of terms in the check list.

A feature adhered to during the construction of this check list may be noticed by examining the statements of the various categories. They show little concern with errors and standards of classroom activity, but provide rather largely for detecting observable facts of classroom activity. In this respect the check list includes considerations of the fraction of the class which participated in the various activities, the type of this participation, and the fraction of the lesson devoted to certain activities.

In addition to the check list's value as an instrument of measurement in this study, possibilities for its use as a guide in analyzing the pupil activities in classrooms can be recognized. Either in its present form or in a modified arrangement it can serve in this capacity of detector of specific types of activity programs. The check list is included here to facilitate more ready reference than would be the case if it were placed in the Appendix.

A CHECK LIST FOR THE OBSERVATION OF PUPIL ACTIVITIES IN THE CLASSROOM

Grade observed.................Subject observed............................

Date...............Time..................Number of pupils observed............

Observational technique used..

Observer's name..................Teacher's name....................

DIRECTIONS: This list of multiple choice items is for the use of observers when they are making their interpretations of the classroom activities after the lesson is concluded. Interpretations of the observed lesson are to be made mainly upon the basis of the pupils' participation by means of their audible oral responses and their use of tangible classroom material. All categories are to be judged independently of each other, i.e., the marking of an item under one category is not to be construed as determining the marking of items in other categories. Each is judged according to the reading of its category heading. Each is judged on the basis of what occurs during the observed lesson. No single item in a category is necessarily to be considered as the only one that is correct educationally. The letters, a, b, c, d, e, on the right margin have no significance for the marking of items. Mark the most appropriate answer in each category of items by placing a cross (X) within the parentheses that precede it. Italics are used to stress the main significance of each category, but the whole statement should be understood clearly before marking the most appropriate answer. Mark one answer and only one in each group.

I. The pupils' *individual answers*, either voluntary or when called upon, *showed* that *thinking or reasoning* in addition to the recall of facts or of drilled responses was involved in approximately
  ( ) less than ¼ of the answers   a
  ( ) ¼ to ½ of the answers   b
  ( ) ½ to ¾ of the answers   c
  ( ) ¾ to all of the answers   d

II. *Questions were answered*, either voluntarily or when called upon, by approximately
  ( ) none to ¼ of the class   a
  ( ) ¼ to ½ of the class   b
  ( ) ½ to ¾ of the class   c
  ( ) ¾ to the whole of the class   d

III. The pupils' *individual oral contributions, other than answers* to questions, were *most frequently*
  ( ) questioning either the teacher or other pupils   a
  ( ) giving reports of individual or small group activities or of committees   b
  ( ) volunteering contributions that were not directly called forth by questions   c
  ( ) dramatizing a play or reading printed material   d

IV. *Oral contributions, other than answers* to questions, i.e., all other responses not previously included under Roman numeral II, were made by approximately
  ( ) none to ¼ of the class   a
  ( ) ¼ to ½ of the class   b
  ( ) ½ to ¾ of the class   c
  ( ) ¾ to the whole of the class   d

A CHECK LIST FOR THE OBSERVATION OF PUPIL ACTIVITIES IN THE CLASSROOM—*Con't*

V. The *questions that were asked by pupils showed* that *reasoning information* in addition to the recall of factual information was requested in approximately
   ( ) ¾ or more of the questions   a
   ( ) ½ to ¾ of the questions   b
   ( ) ¼ to ½ of the questions   c
   ( ) less than ¼ of the questions   d

VI. *Questions of any kind were asked* by approximately
   ( ) none to ¼ of the class   a
   ( ) ¼ to ½ of the class   b
   ( ) ½ to ¾ of the class   c
   ( ) ¾ to the whole of the class   d

VII. The *material which the pupils used the most* or mentioned using the most was
   ( ) *class textbook*   a
   ( ) *reference or supplementary* books or printed material other than class textbook   b
   ( ) *illustrative* material such as maps, models, apparatus, constructive material, pictures, drawings, or charts that illustrated the lesson; this might have included illustrations on the blackboard if referred to *by pupils*   c
   ( ) material that *measured pupil progress*, such as tests, graphs, or rating scales; this might have included measures of pupil progress on the blackboard if referred to *by pupils*   d
   ( ) *practice or drill* material, such as mimeographed or printed sheets, workbooks, outlines, practice or drill cards; this might have included practice on the blackboard or on typewriters if used *by pupils*   e

VIII. *Tangible classroom material of any kind was used* or was mentioned as being used by approximately
   ( ) none to ¼ of the class   a
   ( ) ¼ to ½ of the class   b
   ( ) ½ to ¾ of the class   c
   ( ) ¾ to the whole of the class   d

IX. The *provision for the pupils' individual differences*, as distinct from class work or class discussion in which all pupils were doing the same things or discussing the same topics, showed that there was evidence of some distinctly individual or small group work or reports of such work during approximately
   ( ) ¾ or more of the whole lesson   a
   ( ) ½ to ¾ of the whole lesson   b
   ( ) ¼ to ½ of the whole lesson   c
   ( ) less than ¼ of the whole lesson   d

X. The *pupils that participated during this lesson in any distinctly individual or small group work* or in reporting such work, as distinct from class work or class discussion in which all pupils were doing the same things or discussing the same topics, included approximately
   ( ) none to ¼ of the class   a
   ( ) ¼ to ½ of the class   b
   ( ) ½ to ¾ of the class   c
   ( ) ¾ to the whole of the class   d

A Check List for the Observation of Pupil Activities in the Classroom—*Con't*

XI. The *most information for the teacher in regard to the progress of the greatest number of pupils would be expected to result from*
( ) pupils getting actual *measures of their progress* through test, scale, graph, or norm   a
( ) *oral reasoning* or thinking in addition to the recall of factual information during pupil recitation, discussion, or reports   b
( ) *oral recall* of factual information during pupil recitation, discussion, or reports   c
( ) *written practice or written drill* material that directed study, or that was intended to improve the pupils' abilities in the subject of the lesson   d

XII. The *use of any oral or material means* that would be expected *to indicate the pupils' progress* was evidenced by approximately
( ) none to ¼ of the class   a
( ) ¼ to ½ of the class   b
( ) ½ to ¾ of the class   c
( ) ¾ to the whole of the class   d

XIII. The *type of activities in which the pupils utilized most of the lesson time* was
( ) *individual or small group* rather than class activities   a
( ) *class* activities that were aesthetic, dramatic, or artistic, and *which emphasized individual appreciation* rather than socialized discussion   b
( ) *class* activities allowing considerable oral expression of the pupils' thoughts by means of *socialized recitation or discussion*   c
( ) *formal class-questioning* by the teacher and answering by the pupils   d
( ) almost wholly *directed class* activities, *such as practice* or drill in studying, analyzing, reasoning, or note-taking   e

XIV. The pupils' *participation, either orally* during activities in which the pupils of the class were expected to participate *or through the use of any tangible classroom material,* involved approximately
( ) none to ¼ of the class   a
( ) ¼ to ½ of the class   b
( ) ½ to ¾ of the class   c
( ) ¾ to the whole of the class   d

XV. The pupils' *relation to the assignment or to suggestions for future study,* either as received from the teacher or as decided upon during this lesson, showed that the pupils
( ) *neither received* any from the teacher *nor decided* upon any during class work   a
( ) *received or decided* assignments *in small groups* or in committees   b
( ) *received or decided upon a statement* of the problem, topic, or pages to be "taken up" by the class but there was *no suggestion for further* class *study* or for small group assignments   c
( ) *received or decided upon definite suggestions for further class study* but there were *no small group assignments*   d
( ) *received or decided assignments as individuals*   e

XVI. A *fairly clear understanding of how to participate in the work* or activity of this lesson, as was shown by means of what the pupils said or by the way in which they used material, was had by approximately
( ) none to ¼ of the class   a
( ) ¼ to ½ of the class   b
( ) ½ to ¾ of the class   c
( ) ¾ to the whole of the class   d

A CHECK LIST FOR THE OBSERVATION OF PUPIL ACTIVITIES IN THE CLASSROOM—*Con't*

XVII. *No oral participation of any kind* during activities in which the pupils of the class were expected to participate was evidenced by approximately
( ) none to ¼ of the class   a
( ) ¼ to ½ of the class   b
( ) ½ to ¾ of the class   c
( ) ¾ to the whole of the class   d

XVIII. The *majority of the pupils showed* the extent of their *abilities to act independently* in their classroom work by
( ) about half of the time being self-reliant and self-confident; about half of the time expressing their thoughts clearly   a
( ) always being self-confident and sure of themselves; excellent expression of their thoughts   b
( ) being very dependent and subservient; expressing their thoughts poorly   c
( ) usually working well independently and meeting difficulties with poise; usually expressing their thoughts clearly   d
( ) frequently being disconcerted and inclined toward subservience; less than half of the time expressing their thoughts clearly   e

XIX. The *evidences of the pupils' planning* whereby they arranged beforehand for activities that occurred during the lesson or for activities that will occur in future lessons showed
( ) a predominance of *cooperative planning* for the activities of the class or of groups of pupils   a
( ) pupil-planning almost entirely *teacher-dominated* rather than teacher-guided   b
( ) a predominance of *individual planning* for the respective activities of each pupil   c
( ) practically *no pupil-planning*   d

XX. *Situations in which choices by the pupils were most numerous* involved the choosing of
( ) *tangible classroom material*   a
( ) other *pupils* who carried on an activity or who participated with them in small groups or committees   b
( ) *no choosing* of any kind by the pupils   c
( ) any *activity other than* the choice of tangible classroom material or of pupils   d

XXI. The *most frequent way* in which the activities provided *for the pupils' growth in knowledge, appreciation, or skill* was through the development of
( ) *research technique* by means of the pupils' gathering of information from various sources with the intention of formulating new ideas, relationships, or generalizations; the pupils had one or more topics to study   a
( ) *knowledge by means other than the pupils' own research;* the pupils were formulating new ideas, relationships, or generalizations by means other than the research technique stated above   b
( ) *appreciation* of aesthetic, dramatic, or artistic value   c
( ) *practice or drill* through the repetition of similar types of exercises or skills   d

XXII. The *pupils' experiences outside of the classroom* that were *most frequently mentioned* in relation to their classroom activities were
( ) *home experiences*   a
( ) *community or city experiences* that were outside of the home   b
( ) *experiences* outside of the classroom were *not mentioned*   c
( ) *experiences beyond their community or city*   d

A CHECK LIST FOR THE OBSERVATION OF PUPIL ACTIVITIES IN THE CLASSROOM—*Con't*

XXIII.　The *most frequent evidence pertaining to the pupils' ability to use any tangible classroom material* showed that

( )　*no materials were provided* for the pupils' use　　　　　　　　　a

( )　most pupils were *using effectively* the materials that were provided for them　　　　　　　　　b

( )　most pupils were *not using materials when needed although these were provided* for them　　　　　　　　　c

( )　most pupils were in *need of training in the proper use* of the materials that were provided for them　　　　　　　　　d

XXIV.　The *majority of the pupils showed* by their attitudes of *consideration and respect* that they were

( )　usually considerate of others' welfare and respectful of others' opinions; usually willing to comply reasonably with the suggestions from authority　　　　　　　　　a

( )　always permitting personal desires to dominate their consideration for others' welfare and their respect for others' opinions; very frequently unwilling to comply reasonably with the suggestions from authority　　　　　　　　　b

( )　always very considerate of others' welfare and very respectful of others' opinions; always willing to comply reasonably with the suggestions from authority　　　　　　　　　c

( )　frequently inconsiderate of others' welfare and indifferent toward others' opinions; somewhat unwilling to comply reasonably with the suggestions from authority　　　　　　　　　d

( )　about half of the time considerate of others' welfare and respectful of others' opinions; about half of the time willing to comply reasonably with the suggestions from authority　　　　　　　　　e

XXVa.　On the basis of what you saw and heard, state very briefly what you consider was the *major objective or aim of this lesson:*

XXVb.　The *major objective of this lesson as you have written it* above was evidently

( )　only partially or slightly accomplished by the majority of the pupils　　a

( )　in the process of formulation by the majority of the pupils　　b

( )　very indefinite or ambiguous to the majority of the pupils　　c

( )　almost fully accomplished or entirely accomplished by the majority of the pupils　　d

EXPLANATIONS OF TERMS IN
A CHECK LIST FOR THE OBSERVATION OF PUPIL
ACTIVITIES IN THE CLASSROOM

Categories I to XVI, inclusive, are paired so that a category describing an activity is followed by a category estimating the fraction of the class that is participating in a similar activity.

Audible oral responses, used in the directions that precede the check list items, means spoken so that the actual words or numbers can be heard; they include responses spoken in group work as well as in class work.

Tangible classroom material, used in directions and in categories VIII, XIV, XX, and XXIII, means anything used by the pupils within classrooms except things involved in such routine as passing or collecting papers, using wastebasket, erasing blackboard, or using chair or desk.

Or, as used in any of the categories, may mean "and" as well as "or."

Answers, used in category I: When an answer is given in terms of figures or by a word or two, the decision rests upon whether that answer was made more as a result of the recall of a fact or more as a result of thinking or reasoning with facts. This decision does not involve consideration of the correctness of the answer.

Answered, used in category II, does not involve consideration of the correctness of the answer.

Small group, used in categories III, IX, X, XIII, XV, XX, and XXVb, means generally the grouping of from two to four pupils, but would never exceed a third of the pupils in the whole class.

Class, used in categories IX, X, XIII, and XV, means a group that includes more than a third of the whole number of pupils.

Class textbook, used in category VII: Announcement would be made previous to the demonstration if a class were to use the same textbooks.

Used, used in categories VII, VIII, and XVI, means the actual personal use of tangible classroom material.

Provision for individual differences, used in category IX, means any evidence of individual or small group work or reports of such work by pupils. It does not mean provision for individual differences in class work.

Pupils of the class were expected to participate, used in categories XIV and XVII, means any oral activities including individual, group, and class activities with the exception of oral participation that has no evident relation to the work or subject of the lesson, or to an oral response that shows the pupil is not attempting to answer a question that he has been asked.

Mentioned, used in category XXII, means actual pupil-experiences or likely pupil-experiences mentioned either by the teacher or by the pupils. In addition to the pupils' personal contacts, these experiences might have come through other sources, such as radio, theater, or reading.

CHAPTER IV

Descriptive Account of Experimental
Arrangements' and Procedure

Grouping of observers. As there were four prevalent observational techniques to be investigated, the one hundred and thirty-six students who were in training to become teachers were divided into four groups of observers. Before a comparison of the observational techniques was made, the four groups were equated on the basis of their abilities to observe lessons. This was accomplished by means of three preliminary lessons which the students observed without making any records of data until the conclusion of each lesson, when all marked the check list. In order that they might become familiar with its contents, the check list was distributed to the students a week prior to the first preliminary lesson. Table 3 shows the mean scores of the equated groups and also the standard deviations. It is evident from the data of this table that the groups were very closely equated.

Table 3

MEAN SCORE AND STANDARD DEVIATION FOR FOUR OBSERVATIONAL GROUPS
EQUATED ACCORDING TO SCORES ON THE CHECK LIST

	Group I	Group II	Group III	Group IV
Mean score..................	11.32	11.32	11.29	11.32
Standard deviation...........	2.59	2.45	2.74	2.61
Number of student-teachers....	34	34	34	34

The techniques of observation assigned to the four groups were: *no record* technique to group I, *running notes* technique to group II, *code* and seating chart technique to group III, and same *code* and seating chart *plus* the additional knowledge of the *teacher's objective* technique to group IV. The teachers' objectives for the ten observed lessons are included in Appendix A.

During these preliminary lessons the seating of observers was arranged so that an equal number in each group had similar locations in the balcony of the demonstration room. This permitted each group to see and hear without discrimination what was taking place during the lessons. The same seating precaution was taken at the beginning of the lessons included in the main part of the experiment.

Observees. Classes of pupils enrolled in the fourth, fifth, and sixth grades of a public school in Providence were the observees. This school is the state demonstration school of Rhode Island College of Education. Its faculty consists of experienced teachers who frequently conduct their lessons in the demonstration room for the benefit of college students who are observing. For the purpose of this study, four of these teachers taught their own regular classes of twenty-four pupils each in this room. It is readily recognized that only children and teachers who are thoroughly used to being observed by large groups would be suitable observees.

Judges. Five members of the college faculty, observing the same lessons that were observed by the four groups of college students, acted in the capacity of judges. Their marking of the same check list that was used at the conclusion of each lesson by student observers, established a criterion by which the accuracy of the students' marking could be determined. To assist the judges in making their decisions stenographic records of everything said by pupils and teachers were given them to review prior to their marking of the check list. A highly efficient stenographer having courtroom experience was engaged for this work. She sat in the first row of the balcony and had the assistance of one who knew all the pupils' names. As each child spoke, the assistant pointed to his name on a seating chart of the classroom. These records are presented in Appendix B. Among the authors who have emphasized the value of stenographic records of lessons are Mead [28 : 1930], Blackhurst [9 : 1925], Anderson, Barr, and Bush [8 : 1925], and Hillegas and Lewis [20 : 1924]. Two additional observers who were graduate students recorded the pupils' use of materials, and this information was also placed at the judges' disposal. These observers memorized the following code pertaining to the pupils' use of materials:

CODE SHOWING USE OR MENTION OF USE OF CLASSROOM MATERIAL BY PUPILS

t—class textbook.

s—supplementary or reference book or printed material other than class textbook.

i—illustrative material, such as map, model, apparatus, constructive material, picture, drawing, or chart (also illustrations on blackboard if referred to by pupil).

m—material that measured pupil progress, such as test, graph, or rating scale (also measures of pupil progress on blackboard if referred to by pupil).

d—drill material, such as mimeographed or printed sheets, workbook, outline, practice or drill cards (also practice on the blackboard if used by pupil).

Directions: Write codes in seating-chart spaces to indicate pupils that are using material for individual or small-group or committee work. Draw a circle around codes when pupils are working with the material in a small group or committee. Write codes under the whole seating chart when the material is being used by the whole class.

The validity of the judges' opinions was increased in each lesson by the elimination of any category in the check list where fewer than four of five judges concurred in their marking of items.

Observation of ten lessons. Following the three preliminary observations, ten lessons were observed by the four groups of students, each group using a different observational technique, as outlined at the beginning of this chapter. The check list that all observers marked at the conclusion of each lesson was scored by counting the number of categories in which the proper subitems were checked. The proper item to be checked was in all cases the one checked by the judges as explained above. The observers' interest in their marking of the check lists was retained by informing them of the judges' markings as soon as all five judges had returned their decisions after each lesson. By comparing choices of items in this way, observers were in a position to know where their differences were occurring and thereby attempt in the next lessons to observe more carefully in the categories concerned. Through this information received between lessons, the subject-content was rotated so that social studies followed English and arithmetic followed social studies. Similarly, the teachers of the lessons were rotated so that none taught two consecutive lessons nor the same subject twice. Classes as well as teachers presented their lessons in rotating order. This plan eliminated the advantage to observers that might develop through practice effect resulting from becoming more accustomed to one class or to one subject than to the others at any time during the experiment.

Directions given to observers. Prior to each of the three preliminary lessons and to the first of the ten experimental lessons, specific directions were given observers in order to assure their complete understanding of the use of terms, seating arrangements, and the procedures involved in executing the study. A complete stenographic record was made of these directions and comments. This will be presented here to give a detailed picture of the investigation's procedure.

DIRECTIONS GIVEN AT THE TIME OF THE CHECK LISTS'
DISTRIBUTION ONE WEEK PRIOR TO THE
FIRST PRELIMINARY OBSERVATION

Types of Recording Techniques:

After this week you are going to observe classes of pupils by somewhat different means than you have used heretofore. Up to the present time you have done undirected observation, but now your observation will be directed by the guide called, *A Check List for the Observation of Pupil Activities in the Classroom,* which you have just received. Become familiar with its contents so that you will know what to look for during the coming observations. These Check Lists will be marked by you at the conclusion of each lesson.

While the next three lessons are in progress you will observe without using any recording form during the observations. Later you will have observations in which different observers will use different observational techniques during the progress of the lessons. Some of you will make full running notes of everything that occurs during the lesson. Others will use a code with a seating-plan of the pupils. These observers will have the code memorized in order that they can write the proper codes on the seating-plan as soon as the pupils' comments are made. Other observers will have knowledge of the teacher's lesson-objective prior to the beginning of each observation. Eventually, the four types of observational techniques that will be used during observations will be: I. No Record; II. Full Running Notes; III. Code with Seating-plan of the Pupils; and IV. Code with Seating-plan and the additional knowledge of the Teacher's Objective of the Lesson.

Purpose of These Procedures:

Probably you would like to know the purpose of these procedures. It is to determine some of the values obtained through use of certain observational techniques. This Check List will be marked by everyone regardless of which observational technique is used. While this is being done, there must be no conversation nor collaboration. There must be full cooperation from everyone in this respect. You will mark one and only one item under each category. (Roman numerals indicate categories.) The choices that you make will be tabulated in group form so that the emphasis will be upon your scores as a group and not upon your individual scores.

Most Appropriate Multiple-Choice Items:

Note that after each category there are a number of choices. You are familiar with the multiple-choice type of questionnaire. You will want to know from week to week how closely your choices come to the faculty decisions; therefore, after each observation you will be notified on the bulletin board what the most appropriate choices were. In this way you will know how closely you come to being experienced judges of the lessons. Prior to the next observation you will get another of these forms. You will take this one with you to review carefully before the next observation. So that you can have a duplicate Check List to refer to when comparing your choices with those of the faculty, you can use the letters at the right edge of the form. Keep such a reference Check List throughout the series of observations by adding after each the item-letters of the multiple choices that you considered most appropriate to the lesson.

Directions for Checking Category-Items:

Look at the first category on the Check List. There are four items. Suppose that you think from one-half to three-fourths of the answers showed thinking in addition to the recall of facts, what item-letter on the right margin would represent the proper choice?

Students: "c."

Before the next observation the results of the faculty choices will be put on the board and you will see whether "c" was the right choice. At another observation let us suppose that one-fourth of the answers showed thinking; what letter would be chosen?

Students: "b."

Is there any question about that? You will notice that the emphasis throughout the Check List is upon the pupils' activities. Look at category II. Imagine that there were 24 pupils in the class. How many pupils would be included under the first item which reads "none to $\frac{1}{4}$ of the class"?

Students: "6."

No, 0-5 inclusive. Notice the statement reads "to $\frac{1}{4}$ of the class." The next item reads "$\frac{1}{4}$ to $\frac{1}{2}$ of the class."

Students: "6-11 inclusive."

Yes, and the next is "$\frac{1}{2}$ to $\frac{3}{4}$ of the class."

Students: "12-17 inclusive."

And the last item, "$\frac{3}{4}$ to the whole class."

Students: "18-24 inclusive."

Don't think that you are expected to know exactly the number that answered questions unless in later observations you are given some means of accurately determining this. Use your best judgment. Items are worded this way in order to have a definite instrument of measurement. Do you, Professor (Judge), think these directions are clear?

Professor (Judge): "Yes."

Do you, Dr. (Judge)?

Dr. (Judge): "Yes."

Read the directions on the first page of the Check List to see if there is any statement that is not clear.

Definition of Terms in the Check List:

Look at the typed sheet that is attached to the Check List. It is entitled, *Explanations of Terms that occur in A Check List for the Observation of Pupil Activities in the Classroom.* We shall read each definition and discuss any needing further clarification:

Tangible classroom material, used in directions and in categories VIII, XIV, XX, and XXIII, refers to instructional material such as books, maps, pictures, apparatus, charts, graphs, etc. It does not refer to notes or papers written by the pupils.

As an example of the definition of *or*, look at category I which reads, "The pupils' individual answers, either voluntary or when called upon." Since by definition this word may mean "and" as well as "or," you will not need to decide whether it is a voluntary answer or a drafted answer (pupil called on). Both are included.

The term, *answers*, also occurs in category I. You are asked to differentiate between answers showing thinking or reasoning and those showing recall of facts or drilled responses. If a pupil uses numbers to solve a problem, he is thinking or reasoning in addition to recalling facts. The naming of a State Capital is a recall of a fact or a drilled response; but any discussion of the Capital would probably involve reasoning in addition to the recall of facts. What are these? "It was raining today."

Students: "Recall of fact."

"Two times six is twelve."

Students: "Recall of fact or drilled response."

Under category III the term, *small group*, is mentioned in the second item. Notice what your definition sheet considers a small group of pupils for purposes of using the Check List. As an example—If there were 24 pupils in the class, how large a group could participate together before it got out of a small group and into a class situation?

Students: "8."

Yes, if you observed nine or more pupils participating together, you would have more than a third and would consider that it was class activity.

As an illustration of the definition, *class textbooks*, look at category VII. If it is announced that all the pupils will use the same textbook, does that automatically make you cross the first item under this category?

Student: "No, although the pupils have textbooks, they might not use them the most of all material."

Yes. Questions? Notice in category IX, *provision for individual differences*. If the first item were marked, it would indicate that three-fourths or more of the whole lesson showed something. What?

Student: "It would show that pupils or groups of pupils were working by themselves during three-fourths or more of the whole lesson."

I think you have the right idea. It doesn't have to be the same pupils or same groups that work by themselves or report their work to the class for that length of time. Pupils may be changing from their own activities to class activities, but some individual or group activity would be in evidence by one or more pupils during three-fourths or more of the whole lesson time. Look frequently around the room and see whether you notice a small group or small groups working on something apart from the rest of the class. If during the whole lesson, you observe individual pupils or small groups working at activities distinct from class work as defined in the category, which item would you mark?

Students: "The third one."

If a little less than three-fourths of the whole lesson were given over to class work, thus leaving a little more than one-fourth of the whole lesson that showed evidence of individual or small group work, which item would you mark?

Student: "The third one."

You will notice that in some categories the lowest fraction occurs in the first item while in other categories, the positions are reversed and the highest fraction occurs in the first item. For example, in category I the choice begins with the lowest fraction, viz., *less than* $\frac{1}{4}$ *of the answers.* Then look at category V and you will notice that the choice begins with the highest fraction, viz., $\frac{3}{4}$ *or more of the questions.* Always read carefully the category items in order to be sure which way these statements are arranged.

Category X shows something further about the individual or small group work.

Student: "The number of pupils that participated in individual or small group work."

Yes, and participated at any time during the entire lesson. Also, any pupils reporting such work are included.

The third category asks for the pupils' individual oral contributions other than answers to questions. Notice that the italicized words ask for the most frequent number of contributions; they do not ask the length of time devoted to these contributions. It is the frequency of individual oral contributions and not the gross amount of time devoted to contributions. For example, if two pupils ask two questions and take only a minute's time; and another pupil reads printed material for half an hour, which item would you mark?

Student: "The first item."

Turn to category XVIII where you have five levels of the pupils' abilities to act independently. If the situation showed almost a perfectly desirable condition, which one would you mark?

Student: "b."

That would be an excellent situation. Which item would indicate the next to the best situation?

Student: "d."

Which would be the middle choice?

Student: "a."

The next lower one in rank?

Student: "e."

And the lowest rank?

Student: "c."

Do you, Professor (Judge), want to raise any question?
Professor (Judge): "I can't think of anything now."
Professor (Judge)?
"No."
Dr. (Judge)?
"No."
Professor (Judge)?
"No."

DIRECTIONS PRIOR TO THE FIRST
PRELIMINARY OBSERVATION

Prior to the next observation, you are to change your seats. Those in the back row will sit in the front row; those in the front row will sit in the middle row; and those in the middle row will sit in the back row.

Today none of you will do any writing during the observation. Just observe. There is to be no writing whatever by any student during today's observation.

Under category XIII, which item indicates that during most of the lesson time there was no class activity?

Student: "The first one."

Class activity does not necessarily mean that the children were doing something active. For example, an appreciative audience of pupils would be engaged in listening activities. In these observations class activity means that more than a third of the pupils were giving their attention to the same thing.

In category V, suppose that only one pupil asked a question and that this question showed that reasoning information were requested, which item would you mark?

Student: "a," the first one.

If no questions were asked by pupils, mark the fourth item, "d," under category V.

Under category XVIII, what would you do if few or no pupils expressed their thoughts? You would do your choosing on the basis of their actions, that is, how self-reliant and self-confident did they appear.

Category XX, like the others, is marked on the basis of what happened during the observation rather than on the basis of what happened prior to or subsequent to the lesson.

Has anyone a question regarding the use of terms?

Student: "In the ninth category, doesn't that mean that the teacher gives the pupil special work?"

All you have to look for are evidences of individual or small group work as distinct from class work or class discussion in which more than a third of the pupils were doing the same things. Is that clear? Any other question?

DIRECTIONS PRIOR TO THE SECOND
PRELIMINARY OBSERVATION

This morning we shall review a few things which pertain to the Check List in the light of how you marked the first observation. The directions call for crosses to be placed inside the parentheses, not letters nor check marks.

Mark some item under every category. That may appear difficult in some cases; but there is no discredit if it is the wrong choice. Mark the most likely item in every category.

The fourth category includes all the items in the third category. For example, if there were considerable *dramatizing a play or reading printed material* and considerable *giving reports* so that almost all the pupils of the class contributed, you would cross the last item, ¾ *to the whole of the class.* Category IV is the fraction of the class that did any of the things mentioned under category III.

Under category XXII, do you think that it is a good thing to recall the experiences that pupils have had and to encourage them to draw from their out-of-school experiences during school work?

Student: "Yes, because children learn from their own experiences."

Does anyone recall a definite instance in the last observation?

Student: "The teacher asked the little boy what a shadow was and asked him if he remembered seeing his own shadow."

Many of you marked the item indicating that there was no mention of any experience outside the classroom. You overlooked the experience that was just mentioned. Who can think of another?

Student: "The experience of the echo."

Which item would be crossed for that particular kind?

Student: "d," beyond their community or city."

Does anyone think of another experience?

Student: "Mouse and cat."

Dr. (Judge): "The burrow."

Yes, the teacher thought it doubtful that the pupil would know what a burrow is. That would be another example of an experience outside the home.

We hear much about planning. Why should pupils plan their school activities?

Student: "It emphasizes the aim or purpose of the lesson, and helps the children realize the end in view."

Student: "How can you have a lesson without planning?"

Has anyone anything to say about that?

Student: "What do you mean by pupil planning? How can a very young child plan anything? I mean children in the lower grades."

Student: "I saw a case in the kindergarten. Two children were building a bed. One of them said, 'We shall put this on first, then we shall put the middle one on, and then the last one.' "

Planning often avoids wasting time and energy. We want the pupils to know that in general the more they think before they act, the better act they will do. We had cooperative planning in the last observation. What was the cooperation?

Student: "One took the part of stage manager and I think one was also a character that cooperated on taking the cue."

In regard to writing the major objective or aim of the lesson, it is not expected that any two students will make exactly the same statement. What do you think was the major aim of the teacher in the last observation?

Student: "I thought it was doubly an appreciation lesson."

What type of situation did the pupils want to have?

Student: "A good audience situation."

Do you feel that the lesson was primarily for the benefit of the pupils that read or took part in the plays or do you feel that it was for the benefit of the whole class?

Students: "Whole class."

We interpret it as creating a good audience situation. The teacher's statement of the major objective was, "Appreciation of literature involving eager giving and glad receiving with an opportunity to experience a good audience situation."

We saw an appreciation lesson last week. What other kind might we observe?

Students: "Drill."

Students: "Study lesson."

Students: "Directed study lesson."

Students: "Lecture."

Students: "Discussion and recitation."

What do we mean by a recitation lesson?

Student: "It could be a discussion lesson."

If it is a discussion, what kind of lesson do we usually call it?

Student: "Socialized discussion."

Recitation types of pupil activities range from well-socialized recitations to formed question-answer recitations.

Sometimes lessons are presented in the form of problems or hypotheses. Pupils then study topics dealing with these by looking up references and entering into various other fact-finding activities. This procedure is often called research. What subjects would lend themselves to this type of technique?

Students: "History."

Students: "Geography."

Students: "Chemistry."

Might almost any subject under certain conditions lend itself to this technique? Yes, you couldn't draw lines separating subjects in this respect because almost any subject might present problems involving this type of activity.

DIRECTIONS PRIOR TO THIRD
PRELIMINARY LESSON

The seats that you are occupying for today's observation are temporary ones. Note that the directions on the blackboard state that no one is to sit in the same row nor on the same side of the balcony in which he sat during the last observation. Sign your name in the proper space on the seating charts that are being circulated.

On Friday morning lists of your names will be posted upon the college bulletin board. Your name will appear in one of four groups of names. The groups will be numbered 1, 2, 3, and 4. If your name is in group 3 or in group 4, you are to obtain a paper with a code printed on it. Be sure that you get this code in the office on Friday and that you memorize it prior to next week's observation. You are to know thoroughly the codes and their meanings before coming to the observation next Tuesday. Only members of groups 3 and 4 are to do this.

Today everyone will observe according to the technique that has been used in the previous observations, namely, by not making any records during the observation. Observe carefully so that your marking of the Check Lists after the lesson will be as accurate as possible.

DIRECTIONS PRIOR TO FIRST OF
TEN EXPERIMENTAL OBSERVATIONS

Every observer is to occupy the seat assigned him on the new seating chart. Your number on this chart refers to the observational group to which you have been assigned.

All observers in group IV rise. Take one of the sheets that are being distributed and read the teacher's objective of the lesson which is printed on the bottom of the sheet. Prior to every lesson you are to read and use any help derived from the teacher's objective or aim of the lesson which you will always find on the bottom of your seating chart. Be seated.

All observers in group III rise. Take one of the sheets that are being distributed and then be seated.

All observers in both groups III and IV who have just risen, write on the sheet which you have just received the five codes and their meanings. If anyone has a question to ask concerning the codes please rise. (No questions.)

All observers in group II rise. Take one of the blank sheets that are being distributed. Write on it full running notes concerning everything you see and hear that pertains to the check list. Make your notes as complete as you can. When there are things which pertain particularly to the categories in the check list, you are to make stars or asterisks beside these notes so that your attention will be called especially to them.

All observers in group I will observe in the same manner in which they have previously observed. You are not to use any code system, nor to take any notes.

During or after the observation there is to be no comparing of or looking at the data being collected by others either in code or in running notes. Everyone must use only his own observational technique when checking the most appropriate choices on the Check List. Be sure you make full use of your coded seating charts or your running notes when marking your Check Lists. If you are in groups III or IV, where codes are used, remember that before doing the checking you are to study your codes and count the actual fraction of the class that responds. For example, in category IV you find the sum of the pupils who volunteered, asked questions, gave reports, etc., and then find the fraction of the class that this sum is. For category XVII you find the fraction of the class that showed no participation of any kind.

On the board are the following examples of oral participation in the classroom:

Teacher: Is this answer correct?
John: No, it isn't.
Teacher: Is it too large?
John: Yes, it wouldn't be a sensible answer.
Teacher: What is the trouble with this example?
John: The quotient is too large.
Teacher: Yes, that is correct. Mary?
Mary: Figures should be placed under each other.

The teacher said, "Is this answer correct?"; and John said, "No, it isn't." The code for this answer is a. You would have another a when John said, "Yes, it wouldn't be a sensible answer," because the teacher talked in between John's answers. John gives a third answer, "The quotient is too large," which gives him a third code of a. Next, Mary signifies that she wants to say something, "Figures should be placed under each other." Mary volunteered this response and her code is v. Observers in groups III and IV must use some code every time another oral response is made by any pupil. Observers in group II must make their running notes full by stating the things talked about, the materials used or referred to, and especially anything pertaining to your check list items.

Student: When a pupil gets up in the front and calls on someone else, are you supposed to call that a question? It is not a direct question because he is merely recognizing pupils who want to comment on something.

I don't believe it is a question when a pupil just calls another pupil's name. What would you say, Professor (Judge)?

Professor (Judge): I should think it would not be classed as a question unless he asks information.

Student: If the teacher calls for volunteers and seven or eight pupils stand, would you give each pupil credit or just the one who gives the answer?

Credit would be given in such cases to just the pupil who gives the answer. Is there any other problem or question? (No response.) Guard against checking any items on the basis of what occurred before the observation—consider only what is actually seen or heard. Throughout the rest of the observations you will record your observations according to the technique which you use today. Leave both your check list and your observational sheet, face down, in your seat when you leave."

The observers received no further directions before any of the remaining nine lessons other than a statement that they were to continue observing in the same manner. After every lesson a tabulation was made of all the items checked by each observer, and each of these individual total scores showed the number of categories in which observers agreed with the combined opinion of the judges.

Reliability of the method. In order to study the reliability of the method as a measure of individual students, scores obtained on the two halves of the experiment were correlated. Thus the observers' scores on the first group of five lessons were correlated with their scores on the second group of five lessons. One hundred and thirty-six observers comprised the number of paired cases. The coefficient of correlation, as corrected by application of the Spearman-Brown formula, was .63.

As the markings of the check lists were compiled in quantitative terms, the next chapter will show how the data were subjected to statistical treatment to determine the relative merits of the various observational techniques.

CHAPTER V

Statistical Treatment of Data

Method of comparing groups of observers. The key for the scoring of the check list was the judges' decision on which item under each of the twenty-five categories of the check list was the most appropriate for the lesson observed. Thus, each category was scored either right or wrong, making a possible total score of twenty-five for each lesson. Since there were ten lessons observed, a total of two hundred and fifty responses was made by each of the one hundred and thirty-six students. The total number of records for all observers amounted to thirty-four thousand. Each observer's mean score was computed from his check list markings of the ten lessons. These mean scores were divided into groups on the basis of which of the four observational techniques (described at the beginning of Chapter IV) the students had used.

Since the main purpose of this study is to compare more than two groups of data, the method of analysis of variance was used to determine the significance of their differences. This analysis permits a twofold study of the variation of the total data—first through the variation among the means of the groups, and second through an average of the variation within the groups. The calculations are designed mainly to obtain the sum of squares of the deviations of a set of scores from their mean. To complete the analysis, mean squares are computed in order to estimate the variance in the population that is represented by the experimental data. These are found by dividing the sums of squares by the corresponding degrees of freedom. Table 4 shows the analysis of variance of mean scores of individual students for the four observational techniques used in this study.

Table 4

ANALYSIS OF VARIANCE OF MEAN SCORES OF INDIVIDUAL STUDENTS FOR
FOUR GROUPS USING DIFFERENT OBSERVATIONAL TECHNIQUES

Source of Variation	Degrees of Freedom	Sum of Squares	Mean Square
Total.....................	135	220.5047	1.6334
Among means of groups..............	3	13.3102	4.4367
Within groups........................	132	207.1945	1.5697

Computations for Table 4:

$$\text{Number of groups} = 4$$
$$\text{Number of observers in each group} = 34$$
$$\text{Total number of observers} = 136$$
$$\text{Sum of all scores} = 1{,}998.91$$
$$\text{Correction term } (1{,}998.91)^2/136 = 29{,}379.7146$$
$$\text{Sum of squares of 136 scores} = 29{,}600.2193$$
$$Total \text{ sum of squares} = 29{,}600.2193 - 29{,}379.7146$$
$$= 220.5047$$
$$\text{Sum of squares } between \text{ } means \text{ } of \text{ } groups = (487.49^2 + 490.83^2 + 509.92^2 +$$
$$510.67^2)/34 - 29{,}379.7146$$
$$= 13.3102$$
$$\text{Sum of squares } within \text{ } groups = 220.5047 - 13.3102 = 207.1945$$

Comparison of four groups, each using different observational technique. The calculations of Table 4 show that the *mean square among groups* is greater than the *mean square within groups*. The problem becomes one of determining whether the variation among the group means is enough greater than that within groups to be considered significant, or whether these differences may be ascribed to sampling. This is done by calculating the ratio of the mean square among groups to that within groups. The ratio is designated by F:

$$F = \text{mean square among groups/mean square within groups}$$
$$= 4.4367/1.5697 = 2.83$$

Snedecor's [80 : 1938] table 10.3 is the reference for determining the meaning of the F value. The degrees of freedom for the mean square among groups govern the choice of column in the table, while those for that within groups govern the choice of row. Two values of F are recorded at the intersection of the

Table 5

MEAN SCORES, MEAN SQUARES, AND F VALUES FOR THE ANALYSIS OF VARIANCE REFERENCES OF THIS CHAPTER

Categories on Which Scores Are Based	Group	N	Mean Score	Source of Variation	Mean Square	F	$F_{.05}$	$F_{.01}$
All	No record	34	14.34	Among means	4.437	2.83	2.68	3.94
	Notes	34	14.44	Within groups	1.570			
	Code	34	15.00					
	Code and objective	34	15.02					
All	Non-code	68	14.39	Between means	13.138	8.49	3.92	6.84
	Code	68	15.01	Within groups	1.548			
Pupil-participation	Non-code	68	5.51	Between means	9.598	22.12	3.92	6.84
	Code	68	6.04	Within groups	.434			
Activity type	Non-code	68	8.89	Between means	.190	*0.27	3.92	6.84
	Code	68	8.97	Within groups	.712			
Pupil-participation	No record	34	5.50	Among means	3.207	7.28	2.68	3.94
	Notes	34	5.52	Within groups	.440			
	Code	34	6.06					
	Code and objective	34	6.03					

Activity type	No record	34	8.84	Among means	.140	*0.19	2.68	3.94
	Notes	34	8.94	Within groups	.721			
	Code	34	8.94					
	Code and objective	34	8.99					
Pupil-participation	No record	34	5.50	Between means	.008	*0.02	3.98	7.01
	Notes	34	5.52	Within groups	.353			
Pupil-participation	No record	34	5.50	Between means	5.270	13.78	3.98	7.01
	Code	34	6.06	Within groups	.383			
Pupil-participation	No record	34	5.50	Between means	4.728	11.22	3.98	7.01
	Code and objective	34	6.03	Within groups	.421			
All	Code and objective	34	15.02	Between means	.008	*0.005	3.98	7.01
	Code	34	15.00	Within groups	1.554			
All	Code and objective	34	15.02	Between means	4.696	2.92	3.92	6.84
	Other groups	102	14.59	Within groups	1.611			

* Note that the variation between means is *less* than that within groups, resulting in an F less than 1.

column and row. Using the degrees of freedom in the above analysis, namely, 3 and 132, the two values of F recorded in Snedecor's table are 2.68 and 3.94. The first value corresponds to the 5 per cent point which we shall designate significant as it indicates that a value greater than this would not occur in random sampling more than five times in one hundred trials. The second value corresponds to the 1 per cent point which may be designated highly significant as it indicates that a value greater than this would not occur in random sampling more than once in one hundred trials. The F ratio, 2.83, obtained from the analysis of variance of mean scores of individual students for four groups using different observational techniques is somewhat greater than the 5 per cent point of significance. In other words, a value as great as 2.83 would not occur in random sampling five times in a hundred trials. This statement shows that the four techniques vary significantly among themselves.

Since there is a significant difference among the four observational techniques, it is essential to study this difference. The plan devised for doing this required the analysis of data derived from various combinations of observer-groups, and the division of the check list into two groups of categories, one showing the amount of pupil-participation and the other showing the type of pupil-activity. The manner in which this was done is shown by Table 5, which serves as a guide to further comparisons of group data to be described. The left side of the table outlines for each analysis the categories included, the groups compared, the number of cases, and the mean score of each group. The right side of the table summarizes the results of each of these analyses, and facilitates the recognition of resultant values that show significant differences among the compared groups.

Comparison of code groups with non-code groups. To determine more definitely the cause of the significant difference, a comparison can be made between the mean scores of the combined code groups, namely, III and IV, and of the combined non-code groups, namely, I and II. (See Table 6.)

Table 6

ANALYSIS OF VARIANCE OF MEAN SCORES OF INDIVIDUAL STUDENTS FOR
COMBINED CODE GROUPS AND COMBINED NON-CODE GROUPS

Source of Variation	Degrees of Freedom	Sum of Squares	Mean Square
Total................................	135	220.5047	1.6334
Between means of groups............	1	13.1379	13.1379
Within groups......................	134	207.3668	1.5475

$$F = 13.1379/1.5475 = 8.49$$

Snedecor's F table requires for significance at the .05 level, 3.92, and for significance at the .01 level, 6.84. The value, as great as 8.49, would not occur in random sampling in even one per cent of the trials. This highly significant value, due to the larger mean scores of the combined code groups, can be investigated further by dividing the categories of the check list into two groups: *amount of pupil participation* categories and *type of pupil activity* categories.

Comparison of groups on the basis of amount of pupil participation categories and type of pupil activity categories. All categories pertaining to the fraction of the class that participated in any activity are termed *amount of pupil participation* categories. These are associated with the code that is used by the observers in Groups III and IV. Referring to the check list on page 32, it will be noticed that these categories are numbers II, IV, VI, VIII, X, XII, XIV, XVI and XVII. The sixteen remaining numbers will be referred to as *type of pupil activity* categories. Tables 7 and 8 show the analysis of variance for each of these two sets of categories.

Table 7 shows that in the *pupil participation* categories there is a highly significant difference between the code and non-code groups. On the other hand, Table 8 shows that in the *type of pupil activity* categories there is no significant difference between these same groups. Group scores were actually more uniform than the chance expectation. Since the code is

Table 7

ANALYSIS OF VARIANCE OF MEAN SCORES OF INDIVIDUAL STUDENTS IN PUPIL PARTICIPATION CATEGORIES FOR COMBINED CODE GROUPS AND COMBINED NON-CODE GROUPS

Source of Variation	Degrees of Freedom	Sum of Squares	Mean Square
Total.	135	67.7431	.5018
Between means of groups	1	9.5983	9.5983
Within groups	134	58.1448	.4339

$$F = 9.5983/.4339 = 22.12$$

F table requires for significance 3.92 and for high significance 6.84.

Table 8

ANALYSIS OF VARIANCE OF MEAN SCORES OF INDIVIDUAL STUDENTS IN TYPE OF PUPIL ACTIVITY CATEGORIES FOR COMBINED CODE GROUPS AND COMBINED NON-CODE GROUPS

Source of Variation	Degrees of Freedom	Sum of Squares	Mean Square
Total.	135	95.6186	.7083
Between means of groups	1	.1898	.1898
Within groups	134	95.4288	.7122

$$F = .1898/.7122 = 0.27$$

F table requires for significance 3.92.

related directly to the *pupil participation* categories, the above contrast explains the highly significant difference between the code and non-code groups in Table 6 which included all categories.

Similar results are obtained by comparing the four groups of observers without combining them into code and non-code groups. An analysis of variance of mean scores in the nine *pupil participation* categories for these four groups using different observational techniques gives a highly significant value of 7.28. The required value for significance is 2.68, and for high significance 3.94. The same type of analysis in the sixteen *of pupil activity* categories gives a value of 0.19, but 2.68 is required for significance. Consequently, this investigation reveals clearly that in all categories not depending directly upon the code used in the study, no significant difference in the appraisal of these lessons results because of the type of observational technique employed.

In addition to the study's finding that there is a highly significant difference between the code groups and the non-code groups in the *pupil participation* categories, each code group can be analyzed for this difference by comparing it with one of the non-code groups. The *no record* group was the one used as the control for the comparison after it was determined that no significant difference existed between it and the *running notes* group.

Table 9

RESULTS OF ANALYSIS OF VARIANCE OF MEAN SCORES OF INDIVIDUAL STUDENTS IN PUPIL PARTICIPATION CATEGORIES, COMPARING GROUP I WITH EACH OF THE OTHER THREE GROUPS

Comparison of *No Record* Group with:	F Value	$F_{.05}$ Value for Significance	$F_{.01}$ Value for High Significance
Running notes.	0.02	3.98	7.01
Code.	13.78	3.98	7.01
Code and objective.	11.22	3.98	7.01

Table 9 shows that not only was no significant difference found between the *no record* and the *running notes* group scores in pupil participation categories, but these scores were actually more uniform than the chance expectation. The same table also shows that there was a highly significant difference between the *no record group* and the *code group;* likewise that a highly significant difference existed between the *no record* group and the *code plus objective* group. Thus, the highly significant value is credited to both of the code groups rather than to either one of them.

Comparison of *code group* with *code plus teacher's objective* group. The question of benefit to the observers in this study when supplied with a summary of the teacher's objective prior to each lesson is revealed by analyzing the variance of Group III, *Code,* and Group IV, *Code Plus Teacher's Objective.* The resulting value obtained for F. 0.005, is not significant as 3.98 is required for the 5 per cent point of significance.

By comparing Group IV with a combination of the three other groups, a value of 2.92 is obtained. This is not great enough to meet the requirement for significance, 3.92. The above comparisons show that knowledge of the teacher's objective of the lesson does not have significant effect upon observational ability in this study.

Agreement of judges. The criterion for the comparison of the observer's group scores was the agreement of four or all of the five judges. This formed a valid basis for the study since, in the first place, the suitability of the categories in the check list depended upon the recommendations of authors and supervisors of observational practices, and, in the second place, the choices of the most appropriate items to be checked in the categories depended upon the competency of the judges' decisions. Table 10 gives a detailed account of the number of judges agreeing in each category in each lesson. Whenever less than four of the judges marked the same item, the category in the lesson concerned was eliminated from the study. Therefore, figures showing the number of judges in agreement to be four or five indicate the categories upon which the study was based.

Examination of all the categories in the table shows that in forty-eight of them four judges agreed and in one hundred and sixty-six of them five judges agreed, thereby making it possible to include in the study two hundred and fourteen categories or 85.6 per cent of the total number of two hundred and fifty.

The agreement of each judge with every other judge can be

Table 10

NUMBER OF JUDGES AGREEING IN THE MARKING OF CATEGORIES IN EACH
OF THE TEN LESSONS

Category Number	Number of Judges Agreeing on Lesson:									
	1	2	3	4	5	6	7	8	9	10
I.........	5*	5	3	5	4	2	4	3	4	2
II........	5	5	5	5	5	5	4	5	5	5
III........	4	5	5	5	5	5	5	5	3	5
IV........	2	4	5	5	5	5	5	3	5	5
V.........	5	5	5	5	5	4	5	3	5	4
VI........	5	5	5	5	5	5	5	5	5	5
VII........	5	5	5	5	5	5	5	5	5	5
VIII........	4	2	5	5	4	5	5	4	5	4
IX........	3	5	3	5	4	5	5	4	5	5
X.........	5	5	5	5	5	4	4	5	5	4
XI........	4	5	4	4	5	5	5	5	5	5
XII........	2	2	5	5	2	5	5	5	5	5
XIII........	5	3	5	4	5	3	4	5	5	5
XIV........	5	5	5	5	5	5	5	5	5	5
XV........	5	4	4	4	5	4	4	5	3	5
XVI........	5	5	5	3	4	5	5	5	5	5
XVII........	5	5	4	5	3	5	3	5	5	5
XVIII........	3	4	3	5	3	5	4	3	4	3
XIX........	5	5	5	5	4	2	4	5	3	5
XX........	3	5	5	5	5	5	3	5	4	4
XXI........	2	5	5	5	4	5	5	4	5	5
XXII........	4	3	5	4	2	4	5	3	4	4
XXIII........	3	5	5	5	5	5	5	5	5	5
XXIV........	5	4	5	5	4	5	4	5	4	5
XXV........	3	3	5.	4	5	5	5	5	5	5

* Note that since there were five judges, the figure 5, wherever it occurs, represents their complete agreement.

shown directly by percentages that indicate the proportion of items the two judges marked exactly alike. All items that were included in the data of the study were compared. Representing the five judges by the letters, A, B, C, D, and E, the agreements were: A and B .89, A and C .87, A and D .89, A and E .89, B and C .92, B and D .93, B and E .93, C and D .90, C and E .90, and D and E .92.

In categories where the disagreement was greatest, the judges indicated their uncertainty in interpreting their observations. These uncertainties did not influence the findings of the experiment because the categories in which they occurred were eliminated. However, the following discussion of them shows why the judges disagreed in certain lessons. In category I, two of the judges placed question marks over the words, *thinking* and *reasoning,* indicating that they were unable to dissociate these mental processes from the *recall of facts* or *drilled responses.*

In category IV, lessons one and eight, the judges' opinions were divided in their marking of the number of pupils making *oral contributions, other than answers to questions.* In each of these lessons the judges did not agree on whether there were eleven or twelve pupils participating in this particular activity. In lesson one, their choices showed a division of two and two (and one judge disagreeing with these four) in favor of category-items $\frac{1}{4}$ *to* $\frac{1}{2}$ *of the class* and $\frac{1}{2}$ *to* $\frac{3}{4}$ *of the class.* In lesson two, the judges divided three and two for the same reason. Following the general procedure of the study this category, in the two lessons concerned, was eliminated from the scoring of the groups of observers.

In category VIII, second lesson only, the judges disagreed on whether *tangible classroom material of any kind was used.* One judge's notation explained her marking of the item, *none to* $\frac{1}{4}$ *of the class,* as being "due to some getting books at the end of the lesson but not having time to open them."

In category XII, lessons one, two, and five, the judges questioned whether the *use of any oral or material means* as demonstrated in these particular lessons was indicative of pupil progress.

In category XVIII, the items were arranged as a five-point rating scale to measure the *pupils' abilities to act independently.* Although the judges never varied more than one point from each other on this scale throughout the ten lessons, there were five lessons on which four judges did not agree on the same item out of the five in this category.

In category XIX, lesson six showed practically no pupil-planning. The judges recognized this but were divided in their choices of aspects of this type of planning; two of them marked item *b, pupil planning almost entirely teacher-dominated,* and two marked item *d, practically no pupil-planning.* This category in lesson nine showed a predominance of pupil-planning. All judges recognized this but were divided in their choices of aspects of this type of planning; three of them marked item *a, predominance of cooperative planning,* and two marked item *c, a predominance of individual planning.*

In category XXI of the first lesson, each of the four items was marked by a judge. Although there were no notations concerning this category, it appears that the lesson, being a critical analysis of pupils' compositions, did have aspects of practice and of research in addition to that of appreciation.

In category XXII, lessons two, five, and eight, several judges questioned their choices of items, of knowing definitely where an experience mentioned by a pupil occurred.

No other problems of an interpretative nature were mentioned by the judges, but it is conceivable that certain factors not brought into play in this study might have influenced their interpretations of the lessons. Some of these influences will be discussed in Chapter VI as limitations of the study.

CHAPTER VI

Limitations of the Study

The purpose of this chapter is to indicate limitations of the study in regard to the arrangement of the experiment, the use of the check list, and the attainment of observational conditions in keeping with recognized educational theory.

Arrangement of the experiment as a comparative study of groups of observers. Since the study was a group experiment to compare methods of observing, the ability of individuals to use different methods has not been investigated. It is probable that individuals vary considerably in the manner in which they are able to collect evidence of their observations. The study shows that in each of the four groups there were students who showed proficiency in observational ability, and likewise in each group there were students who made comparatively poor scores. However, since the groups remained constant throughout the study, none of these data can indicate what the individual students might have accomplished by using a method other than the one used by them throughout the study. Therefore, the study does not furnish evidence to show that a technique may be good for certain observers but not for others.

Limitations of the check list's use. It will be recalled that the check list for observing pupil activities was used as a measuring instrument to compare four common methods of observing lessons. This was accomplished mainly by determining the presence and amount of aspects of pupil activities rather than by judging the quality of pupils' learning. The measuring instrument is made up almost wholly of categories describing aspects of learning procedures and of categories showing the quantitative phase of pupil activities. The purpose of this arrangement is to obtain observational data that are as objective as possible. Reference to the check list shows that multiple-choice items to be checked under these categories make allowances in their wording for varying experiences of learning that are in progress during certain periods of pupil activity. Further explanation of the purpose of these categories is included in the directions preceding them on the check list. These include the following three statements:

Interpretations of the observed lesson are to be made mainly upon the basis of the pupils' participation by means of their audible, oral responses and their use of tangible classroom material.

Each category is judged on the basis of what occurs during the observed lesson.

No single item in a category is necessarily to be considered as the only one that is correct educationally.

If it were a main purpose to consider the educational value of the checked items, one's educational philosophy would be the principal basis for determining the appropriateness and quality of the pupils' activities. Because of its arrangement, the check list can be used regardless of the manner in which pupil activities are guided by the teacher. The teacher's ability to guide the learning of the pupils is measured indirectly in the sense that it is reflected through the conduct of the pupils' activities. Activities may be variations of any conduct of learning, commonly expressed through such terminology as traditional, transitional, correlated, integrated, formal, informal, and the like. More explicitly the check list items reveal indications of such aspects of learning activity as: answers showing thinking, most frequent oral contributions other than answers, questions requesting reasoning information, material used the most, provision for pupils' individual differences, most frequent type of pupil activity, assignment or suggestions for future study, ability to act independently in work, pupils' planning, pupils' choices, pupils' experiences outside classroom, pupils' ability to use classroom material, and pupils' consideration and respect for others.

Another limitation in the use of the check list in this study involves the extent of the observational periods. The check list was used to make records following each period of observation. The ten lessons observed in this experiment extended over a period of ten weeks and lasted thirty minutes each. The check list as used was essentially an observational guide for judging only the pupil participation that occurred during restricted periods of observation. Its use did not provide a measurement for the broader setting of observation which would necessitate continuity in observing the same pupils over consecutive and longer periods of time. The latter type of observation would in all probability provide a better picture of the total learning taking place in a group of pupils from hour to hour and from day to day. Only through such a continuous process of close observation of a group of pupils throughout their school day, and outside of school as well, if it were possible, could observers obtain more complete and meaningful data showing the pupils' acquisition of multifarious skills, knowledges, attitudes, and ideals. Therefore, the study is limited because of the observer's lack of extensive acquaintance with the pupils, and lack of observation outside the classroom. Without a reasonable degree of such continuity, it might be difficult for the student to make correct interpretations of his observed data because of the bearing of the pupils' prior activities upon the present ones. However, the check list as used in this study concerns itself almost entirely with the detection and recording of what takes place within the more limited periods of observation.

Fundamentals for providing observation in keeping with recognized educational theory. A question that might well be raised in a study of this type is, "How do student observers understand what is really going on in the classroom?" In order to delve into the meaning of this question, it is necessary to deal with both the mechanical facilities of observation and the development of the student observer's conception of what modern education means. The factors that are involved in this undertaking may be visualized by reviewing some of the principles recognized as fundamental to observation in the field of teacher-education. These generally include the following:

1. Observation of various phases (guidance, health, library, auditorium, and other experiences) and age-levels of education should be provided for students in order that they may have a conception of the school as a whole.
2. Observation should continue over a period of time with each group of pupils in order to see how activities progress and learnings develop.
3. Observation should be supplemented by further data and records to assure more accurate understanding of the pupils by the observer.
4. Observation should provide as complete and impersonal data as possible before its analysis by the students.
5. Observation should generally be preceded and followed by conferences with demonstration teacher or college instructor.
6. Observation by the student should become increasingly scientific through early instruction in the necessary qualities of a trained observer.
7. Observation should be related to the student's knowledge of educational theory and subject matter by means of discussions or courses by college or demonstration school faculty.
8. Observation should include the development of the student's ability to identify various aspects of the pupils' learning activities.

Although these fundamentals of observational practices might be considered as a basic arrangement in harmony with recognized educational theory, there are probably very few professional schools of education that are able to provide such a complete program. Among the reasons for this are the difficulties arising from lack of adequate demonstration school facilities, inadequate staffs to guide and supervise observations, transportation facilities between college and off-campus demonstration schools, inadequate physical facilities of the college or demonstration school (such as demonstration rooms), inadequate amount of time for students to devote to observation in addition to their other requirements, and administrative difficulties in arrangement of schedules. The foregoing review indicates some of the fundamental issues from the standpoint of mechanical facilities in providing needed observational experiences.

Transcending all the fundamental principles of observation is the problem concerning the fusion of the student's observation with the modern conception of learning. A review of some of the aspects of this conception will show the changes that have been taking place in the last few years. The logical treatment of subject matter is giving way to the psychological approach to learning. The domination of a single textbook is giving way to the use of many reference books and materials by pupils. The sole use of the lecture and the question-answer procedures in the classroom are giving way to a variety of challenging interests and experiences inherent in the lives of the pupils. Competition among pupils for individual gain or reward is giving way to cooperative enterprise. Individual progress that depended upon class accomplishments is giving way to goals of attainment based upon analysis of individual efficiency. The study of isolated parts of subject matter is giving way to comprehensive study of whole life problems. The schoolroom of passive and listening pupils is giving way to the schoolroom of active and participating pupils. Unrelated acquisition of information and skills is giving way to functional acquisition. Management of the classroom by fears and threats is giving way to management by democratic principles. The understanding of a pupil on the basis of limited classroom contacts is giving way to the understanding of him on the bases of his previous experiences, present environments, and life-attitudes.

Such complete changes in the professionally educated teacher's viewpoint of modern education naturally make increasingly difficult the attainment of adequate observational experiences on the part of the student-teacher. He does not grow in his power to observe by being a critic of the teacher's work, but by being a student of the learning problems presented by the classroom situation. This calls for extended acquaintance with the pupils and for observations of their non-classroom activities as well.

The use of a demonstration room for conducting the experiment had many advantages for the groups of observers, but it might be considered a less normal setting than classrooms for carrying on the pupils' activities. The effect is probably very slight in view of the frequency with which these pupils and their teachers conducted demonstrations in this room with their own furniture and materials.

Only one of the four groups of observers was acquainted in any way with the teachers' plans and this was in regard to the general objectives of the lessons to be observed. The nature of the observational experiment prohibited full acquaintance with the teachers' daily and unit plans. Although furnishing the outlines of the teachers' objectives of the lessons provided no statistically significant advantage, it is conceivable that more detailed information regarding the entire planning of possible pupil-activities might be helpful in increasing observational ability.

These limitations show that the shortage of the study is due mainly to the observer's inability to see each lesson in its entire and normal setting.

Compromise between theory and practice in observation. Since education is not attained through isolated pieces of information, it is evident that intermittent or periodic observation does not give a complete picture of the total learning that is going on in the classroom. Much additional information must be known about the pupils' previous learning and about their concomitant experiences. These facts bring the realization that desirable observation of the same pupils should extend over a considerable period of time. Although institutions of teacher-education are fully cognizant of this need, they have had to compromise in establishing observational facilities because of difficulties previously mentioned. The limitations in the observational procedure of this study reflect certain compromises that are carried on in these institutions. These include the grouping of student observers, periodic observation, and the use of demonstrations of classroom work. Until such time as the observational practices of student-teachers can be conducted in a more ideal manner in the several respects heretofore mentioned, the writer feels that the present study should have definite utilitarian value.

CHAPTER VII

Summary and Conclusions

The purpose of this investigation was to determine some of the values of the observational techniques used by teachers-in-training when appraising lessons. The need for such a study is apparent when one contemplates the numerous practices in this important aspect of training in the teachers colleges.

Many types of observational research have been conducted for the purpose of studying traits of behavior. This study differs from them by using the observation of behavior as the situation for experimentally comparing the observational techniques used by teachers-in-training. Hence the emphasis of the study is upon the observers rather than upon the observees. Basic to the establishment of a criterion, certain preliminary investigations were conducted. First, a study of the opinions of authors of observational guides and manuals as they pertain to pupil activity only, formed the basis for an observational check list. Second, this check list was refined by means of the criticisms of supervisors of training. The resulting *Check List for the Observation of Pupil Activities in the Classroom* served as a guide sheet or measuring instrument in the form of multiple-choice items. The agreement of qualified judges in deciding which category items in the check list should be marked in each lesson formed the criterion against which observers' check list choices were scored.

One hundred and thirty-six college students were divided into four groups equated on the basis of their check list markings of three preliminary lessons. Each group was assigned a different observational technique as follows: group I, *no record,* group II, *full running notes,* group III, *code,* and group IV, *code plus teachers' objective.* Ten lessons were observed by these groups each using its assigned techniques throughout. These four techniques were found to be the most commonly employed methods of observing in representative teachers colleges and normal schools. The technique used by group IV included the teacher's objective of the lesson in addition to the code as this was found to be the most prevalent guide sheet (aside from directions regarding what to look for in the lesson, the purpose of which was fulfilled by the check list). Each of the ten lessons was taught by an experienced teacher to a class of twenty-four pupils. The subjects presented in the lessons were English, social studies, and arithmetic in grades four, five, and six. Detailed directions were given to observers in regard to technique, check list terminology, and other procedures. Special mention should be made in regard to the situation which made possible an experiment of this type. A classroom having a balcony built for observational purposes and accommodating large numbers of observers was available in the campus demonstration school of a teachers college.

The conclusions derived from the findings of this research follow:

1. This study shows that the total scores of the various groups of observers, classified according to the techniques used, differ among themselves more than is readily accounted for on the basis of random sampling.

2. A comparison of the combined code groups with the combined non-code groups shows a statistically highly significant difference in favor of the code groups.

3. By further comparing the code and non-code groups in *amount of pupil participation* categories only which are directly associated with the code used in this study, a statistically highly significant difference is obtained.

4. In comparing the total scores of the code and non-code groups in only the categories based on *type of pupil activity,* the difference between the scores does not differ more than random sampling alone might account for. A similar finding resulted when all four groups were com-

pared on the basis of *type of pupil activity* categories only.

5. A comparison of group I with each of the other groups using *amount of pupil participation* categories only, shows that groups I and II do not differ more than random sampling alone might account for, while each of groups III and IV, when compared with group I shows a highly significant difference indicating the benefit of the code.

6. In testing the value of the teachers' objective of the lesson which was furnished to observers of group IV, it is found that the total scores (all categories included) do not differ from those of group III, code only, more than random sampling alone might account for.

Although the code as used in this study is superior for observing coded items, there is no significant advantage or disadvantage from its use in observing other items. The above findings show that, with the exception of pupil activities directly dependent upon the code, the four techniques of observing do not differ among themselves sufficiently to be statistically significant.

By investigating the agreement of the judges by categories, it is found that four or all five of the judges agree in two hundred and fourteen categories or 85.6 per cent of the total of two hundred and fifty.

In addition to the above outcomes of the experiment, the check list furnishes a new type of observational guide sheet for student-teachers and also provides the measuring instrument for observational ability in this study. In this way it can be used to analyze the activities of entire classes of pupils from the standpoint of a detector of activity types, rather than from the standpoint of a rating device. The stenographic records and the teachers' objectives of the ten observed lessons are included in the Appendix not only with the thought of assisting in corroborating the study, but also with the hope that they may be found useful by teachers in the field and in training.

Classified Bibliography

STUDENT TEACHING AND OBSERVATION

1. ARMENTROUT, WINFIELD D. "Making Observation Effective for Teachers-in-Training." *Educational Administration and Supervision,* 10 : 287-293, 1924.
2. EVENDEN, EDWARD S. *Summary and Interpretation. National Survey of the Education of Teachers.* Bulletin No. 10, Vol. 6. United States Bureau of Education, 1933.
3. FLOWERS, JOHN GARLAND. *Content of Student-Teaching Courses Designed for the Training of Secondary Teachers in State Teachers Colleges.* Contributions to Education, No. 538. Bureau of Publications, Teachers College, Columbia University, New York, 1932.
4. HENDERSON, ELISHA LANE. *The Organization and Administration of Student-Teaching in State Teachers Colleges.* Contributions to Education, No. 692. Bureau of Publications, Teachers College, Columbia University, New York, 1937.
5. MARSHALL, EDNA M. *Evaluation of Types of Student-Teaching.* Contributions to Education, No. 488. Bureau of Publications, Teachers College, Columbia University, New York, 1932.
6. *National Survey of the Education of Teachers. Teacher Education Curricula.* Bulletin No. 10, Vol. 3. United States Bureau of Education, 1933.
7. WILLIAMS, E. I. F. "Administration of Observation in the Teacher-Training Institutions of United States." *Educational Administration and Supervision,* 8 : 331-342, 1922.

OBSERVATIONAL TECHNIQUES

8. ANDERSON, C. J., BARR, A. S., AND BUSH, M. B. *Visiting the Teacher at Work.* Appleton and Co., New York, 1925.
9. BLACKHURST, J. HERBERT. *Directed Observation and Supervised Teaching.* Ginn and Co., Boston, 1925.
10. BLUME, CLARENCE E. "Techniques in the Measuring of Pupil Attention." *Second Yearbook of the National Conference of Supervisors and Directors of Instruction.* Chap. III, pp. 37-55. Bureau of Publications, Teachers College, Columbia University, New York, 1929.

11. Bott, E. A. and Bott, Helen. "Observation and Training of Fundamental Habits in Young Children." *Genetic Psychology Monograph,* Vol. 4, Chap. 1 and III, July, 1928.
12. Burnham, William H. The Observation of Children at the Worcester Normal School." *Pedagogical Seminary,* 1 : 219-224, 1891.
13. Caille, Ruth Kennedy. *Resistant Behavior of Preschool Children.* Child Development Monograph No. 11. Bureau of Publications, Teachers College, Columbia University, New York, 1933.
14. Eisner, Harry. *The Classroom Teachers' Estimation of Intelligence and Industry of High School Students.* Contributions to Education, No. 726. Bureau of Publications, Teachers College, Columbia University, New York, 1937.
15. Ezekiel, L. F. "Changes in Egocentricity of Nursery School Children." *Child Development,* 2 : 74-75, March-December, 1931.
16. Gesell, Arnold and Thompson, Helen. *Infant Behavior: Its Genesis and Growth.* McGraw-Hill Book Co., Inc., New York, 1934.
17. Goodenough, Florence L. "Measuring Behavior Traits by Means of Repeated Short Samples." *Journal of Juvenile Research,* 12 : 230-235, 1928.
18. Goodenough, Florence L. and Anderson, John E. *Experimental Child Study.* The Century Co., New York, 1931.
19. Hattwick, Berta Weiss. "The Influence of Nursery School Attendance upon the Behavior and Personality of the Preschool Child." *Journal of Experimental Education,* 5 : 180-190, December, 1936.
20. Hillegas, M. B. and Lewis, Mary R. "Some Possible Uses of Stenographic Reports of Lessons." *Teachers College Record,* 25 : 188-202, May, 1924.
21. Jack, Manwell, Mengert, and Others. *Behavior of the Preschool Child.* University of Iowa. Studies in Child Welfare, Vol. 9, No. 3, 1934.
22. Jersild, Arthur T. and Fite, Mary D. "Children's Social Adjustment in Nursery School." *Journal of Experimental Education,* 6 : 161-166, December, 1937.
23. Jersild, Arthur T. and Markey, Frances W. *Conflicts Between Preschool Children.* Child Development Monograph No. 21. Bureau of Publications, Teachers College, Columbia University, New York, 1935.
24. Loomis, Alice Marie. *A Technique for Observing the Social Behavior of Nursery School Children.* Child Development Monograph No. 5. Bureau of Publications, Teachers College, Columbia University, New York, 1931.
25. Malloy, H. "Growth in Social Behavior and Mental Activity after Six Months in the Nursery School." *Child Development,* 6 : 303-309, 1935.

26. MARKEY, FRANCES. *Imaginative Behavior of Preschool Children.* Child Development Monograph No. 18. Bureau of Publications, Teachers College, Columbia University, New York, 1935.

27. MARSTON, LESLIE R. *The Emotions of Young Children.* University of Iowa Studies in Child Welfare, Vol. 3, No. 3, June 1925.

28. MEAD, ARTHUR R. *Supervised Student-Teaching.* Johnson Publishing Co., Richmond, Va., 1930.

29. MUNKRES, ALBERTA. *Personality Studies of Six-Year-Old Children in Classroom Situations.* Contribution to Education No. 681. Bureau of Publications, Teachers College, Columbia University, New York, 1934.

30. MURPHY, LOIS BARCLAY. *Social Behavior and Child Personality.* Columbia University Press, New York, 1937.

31. NELSON, JANET F. *Personality and Intelligence.* Child Development Monograph No. 4. Bureau of Publications, Teachers College, Columbia University, New York, 1931.

32. NEWCOMB, THEODORE M. *The Consistency of Certain Extrovert-Introvert Behavior Patterns in Fifty-one Problem Boys.* Contributions to Education, No. 382. Bureau of Publications, Teachers College, Columbia University, New York, 1929.

33. OLSON, WILLARD C. *The Measurement of Nervous Habits in Normal Children.* University of Minnesota Press, Minneapolis, Minn., 1929.

34. PARTEN, MILDRED B. "Social Participation Among Preschool Children." *Journal of Abnormal and Social Psychology,* 27 : 243-269, 1932-1933.

35. RUGG, HAROLD, KRUGER, LOUISE, AND SONDERGAARD, ARENSA. "A Study of the Language of Kindergarten Children." *Journal of Educational Psychology,* 20 : 1-18, January, 1929.

36. RUST, METTA M. *The Effect of Resistance on Intelligence Test Scores of Young Children.* Child Development Monograph No. 6. Bureau of Publications, Teachers College, Columbia University, New York, 1931.

37. SYMONDS, PERCIVAL M. "Study Habits of High School Pupils as Shown by Close Observation of Contrasted Groups." *Teachers College Record,* 27 : 713-724, April, 1926.

38. THOMAS, DOROTHY SWAINE AND ASSOCIATES. *Some New Techniques for Studying Social Behavior.* Child Development Monograph No. 1. Bureau of Publications, Teachers College, Columbia University, New York, 1929.

39. THOMAS, DOROTHY SWAINE AND OTHERS. *Observational Studies of Social Behavior,* Vol. 1: *Social Behavior Patterns.* Institute of Human Relations, Yale University, New Haven, Conn., 1933.

40. WAGONER, LOUISA C. *Observation of Young Children.* Euthenics Series. McGraw-Hill Book Co., Inc., New York, 1935.

41. WAGONER, LOUISA C. "How to Observe Young Children." *Childhood Education,* 13 : 422-425, May, 1937.

42. WRIGHTSTONE, J. WAYNE. "An Instrument for Measuring Group Discussion and Planning." *Journal of Educational Research,* 27 : 641-650, May, 1934.

43. WRIGHTSTONE, J. WAYNE. "Constructing an Observational Technique." *Teachers College Record,* 37 : 1-9, October, 1935.

44. WRINKLE, WILLIAM L. AND ARMENTROUT, WINFIELD D. *Directed Observation and Teaching in Secondary Schools.* The Macmillan Co., New York, 1932.

OBSERVATIONAL MANUALS AND GUIDE SHEETS

45. ARMENTROUT, WINFIELD D. *The Conduct of Student Teaching in State Teachers Colleges.* Education Series No. 2. Colorado Teachers College, 1927.

46. BARR, A. S. *Some Tentative Standards for the Improvement of Teaching in Secondary Schools.* University of Wisconsin, Department of Education.

47. BLACKHURST, J. HERBERT. *Directed Observation and Supervised Teaching,* Ginn and Co., Boston, 1925.

48. BRIM, O. G. Course of Study as Indicated by the Recitation. Minnesota Rural School Survey.

49. BRUECKNER, LEO J. *Scales for the Rating of Teaching Skill.* Scales based upon four types of teaching methods classified by S. A. Courtis, 1930.

50. CONNOR, WILLIAM L. "A New Method of Rating Teachers." *Journal of Educational Research,* 1 : 338-358, January-May, 1920.

51. DAILY, BENJAMIN W. *Handbook and Manual for Student Teaching,* Part II. State Teachers College, West Chester, Pa., 1932.

52. DIEMER, GEORGE AND MELCHER, GEORGE AND ASSOCIATES. *Observations, Participation, and Practice Teaching.* Teachers College of Kansas City. Bulletin, No. 18, 1932.

53. FITZPATRICK, F. BURKE. *Evaluating the Recitation.* Radford State Teachers College, East Radford, Va.

54. FLOWERS, J. J. *Observation of Teaching. A Manual for the Guidance of Teachers-in-Training.* East Texas State Teachers College, Commerce, Texas, 1926.

55. HOPKINS, GEORGE W. *Outlines for Observation.* Western Maryland College, 1924. Westminster, Md.

56. JAMAICA TRAINING SCHOOL FOR TEACHERS. *Observation Guides 1-20 Leaflet.* New York City Schools.

57. MEAD, ARTHUR R. *Supervised Student-Teaching.* Johnson Publishing Co., Richmond, Va., 1930.

58. MICHIGAN STATE NORMAL COLLEGE. *Outlines for Observation.* Ypsilanti, Mich., 1923.

59. MYERS, A. F. AND BEECHEL, E. E. *Manual for Observation and Participation.* Edited by Strayer, George D. American Book Co., New York, 1926.

60. PRYOR, HUGH CLARK. *A Manual for Student Teachers.* Edited by Keith, John A. H. The Macmillan Co., New York, 1931.

61. REEDER, EDWIN H. AND REYNOLDS, ROLLO G. *How to Study a Demonstration Lesson.* (A manual for classroom observation.) Bureau of Publications, Teachers College, Columbia University, New York, 1931.

62. RETAN, GEORGE A. AND ROSS, BLANCHE R. *Outlines for Observation and Conference for Student Teachers.* Edwards Brothers, Inc., Ann Arbor, Mich., 1931.

63. RUSSELL, CHARLES. *A Laboratory Manual for Observation and Participation.* University of the City of Toledo, Ohio, 1924.

64. STRATEMEYER, FLORENCE B. *Provisional Criteria for Evaluating Classroom Activity in the Effective Use of Classroom Materials.* Contributions to Education, No. 460. Bureau of Publications, Teachers College, Columbia University, New York, 1931.

65. DEPARTMENT OF TEACHERS COLLEGES AND NORMAL SCHOOLS. *Observation Form M. G. 98.* Teachers College, Columbia University, New York.

66. *Ibid. Observation Form M. G. 153.* Part I.

67. *Ibid. Observation Form Ed. 136B.*

68. UNIVERSITY OF MICHIGAN SCHOOL OF EDUCATION. *Students Report on Directed Observation.*

69. UNIVERSITY OF TEXAS DEPARTMENT OF EDUCATION. *Observation Record.*

EDUCATIONAL MEASUREMENTS AND STATISTICAL METHODS

70. BRUECKNER, LEO J. "Diagnostic Analysis of Classroom Procedures." *The Elementary School Journal,* 27 : 25-40, September, 1926.

71. COLLINGS, ELLSWORTH. "A Conduct Scale for the Measurement of Teaching." *Journal of Educational Method,* 6 : 97-103, November, 1926.

72. CONNOR, WILLIAM L. "A New Method of Rating Teachers." *Journal of Educational Research,* 1 : 338-358, January-May, 1920.

73. FISHER, R. A. *Statistical Methods for Research Workers.* Oliver and Boyd, Edinburgh, Fourth revised edition, 1933.

74. GARRETT, HENRY E. *Statistics in Psychology and Education.* Longmans, Green and Co., New York, 1926.

75. GATES, ARTHUR I. *Psychology for Students of Education.* The Macmillan Co., New York, 1932.

76. HERRING, JOHN P. "Educative Control by Means of a New Type of Measurement." *Journal of Educational Method,* 4 : 94-103, November, 1924.

77. MONROE, WALTER S. AND CLARK, JOHN A. *Measuring Teaching Efficiency.* Educational Research Circular. University of Illinois Bulletin, Vol. 21, No. 22, January, 1924.

78. PUCKETT, ROSWELL. "Making Supervision Objective." *School Review,* 36 : 209-212, January-December, 1928.

79. SNEDECOR, GEORGE W. *Calculations and Interpretations of Analysis of Variance.* Collegiate Press, Inc., Ames, Iowa, 1934.

80. SNEDECOR, GEORGE W. *Statistical Methods.* Collegiate Press, Inc., Ames, Iowa, 1938.

81. SYMONDS, PERCIVAL M. *Diagnosing Personality and Conduct.* The Century Co., New York, 1931.

82. THURSTONE, LOUIS LEON. *The Reliability and Validity of Tests.* Edwards Brothers, Inc., Ann Arbor, Mich., 1931.

83. WALKER, HELEN M. "The Sampling Problem in Educational Research." *Teachers College Record,* 30 : 760-774, May, 1929.

84. WALKER, HELEN M. *The Measurement of Teaching Efficiency.* Editor's Preface. The Macmillan Co., New York, 1935.

85. WRIGHTSTONE, J. WAYNE. "Measuring Teacher Conduct of Class Discussion." *Elementary School Journal,* 34 : 454-460, February, 1934.

INSTRUCTIONAL MATERIALS

86. BLAISDELL, ALBERT F. AND BALL, FRANCIS E. *American History Story Book.* Little, Brown and Co., 1912.

87. CLARK, JOHN R., OTIS, ARTHUR S., HATTON, CAROLINE. *Modern School Arithmetic, Book V.* World Book Co., Yonkers-on-Hudson, N. Y., 1937.

88. GORDY, WILBUR F. *Stories of Early American History.* Charles Scribner's Sons, New York, 1913.

89. McCALL, WILLIAM A. AND CRABBS, LELAH MAE. *Standard Test Lessons in Reading, Book III.* Bureau of Publications, Teachers College, Columbia University, New York, 1925.

90. NATIONAL SOCIETY FOR THE STUDY OF EDUCATION. *Thirty-second Year Book.* Public School Publishing Co., Bloomington, Ill., 1933.

91. TUCKER, L. E. AND RYAN, E. I. *Historical Plays of Colonial Days.* Longmans, Green and Co., New York, 1927.

APPENDIX

Teachers' Objectives for the Ten Observed Lessons

LESSON 1. ENGLISH

GRADE 5

Learning to Write Through Reading

We are learning to write stories with definite plots. In preparation we have read and analyzed several stories from our fifth grade reading books and discussed other stories familiar to the group.

In each case we have formulated a statement telling what we believe the author was trying to show. Next, we have talked over the setting, characters, and incidents which the author has used to build up his plot. The high point or climax of each story has been found, and the incidents used to bring the story to an end.

Using this background each child has planned and written his own story which will be read to the class for the first time during this period. The class will see in what measure each reader has applied his knowledge of story writing.

LESSON 2. SOCIAL STUDIES

GRADE 4

Introducing a Desert Country

Immediate Aim:

Introducing a new Social Study Unit, principally geographical, concerning how people live in hot, dry lands and what factors in the environment are related to their ways of living.

Two previous regions studied by these pupils were Antarctica and the Amazon Valley.

General Aims:

To promote a sympathetic understanding of the conditions and problems of peoples of other countries in relation to the kinds of lands in which they live.

To give pupils a knowledge of the location and character of the leading surface features of the earth, such as continents, oceans, rivers, plains, mountains, cities, etc., in their relationships to human activity, but not as isolated facts.

Specific Aims:

To recognize simple, direct relationships between ways of living concerned with food, clothing, shelter, travel, and the natural environment.

To understand how factors in the environment help to explain human activities.

To gain a whole-world concept to help pupils to realize the transitions that occur between the equator and the poles.

To show that people live differently according to places in which they live.

To give training in use of simple maps, pictures, and reading material which includes necessary terms and information at the level of the child's comprehension.

LESSON 3. ARITHMETIC

GRADE 4

Drill of Fundamental Number Facts

The major objective of this lesson is to strengthen by means of self-drill the pupils' knowledge of the fundamental facts in multiplication and division. Through the use of fundamental processes and diagnostic material, pupils cultivate a desire to discover their own needs. The material that is provided enables pupils to correct their work as soon as possible.

An effort is made to provide for individual differences in the following ways:

1. Varying the time in which pupils are allowed to complete their work.
2. Varying the amount of the work required.
3. Varying the method of learning.

Care must be taken not to sacrifice accuracy to speed.

LESSON 4. ENGLISH

GRADE 6

Formulating Standards for Written Expression

The major objective of this lesson is to promote in pupils a feeling that they can appreciate and use various types of expression to develop their social, emotional, and intellectual growth. Such English work provides opportunities for them to explore their needs, interests, and abilities through flexible but specific activities. Compositions to be read include Exposition, Narrative, Biography, Description, Poetry, and Friendly Letter. Certain suggested practices guide the pupils during the writing. In this way standards are formed and these lead to self-criticism and further improvement. The group chairmen will mention some of these.

LESSON 5. SOCIAL STUDIES

GRADE 5

Pupil Reports Concerning Production and Geography of California

As the West Indies were first discovered and explored by Europeans they were discussed first. The names of explorers were learned, and stories of their lives were studied. Our attention was then centered upon the things that these men found, such as the land itself, and the forms of life it supported. Since the region is peculiarly rich in unusual physical phenomena, much time was taken to find the reasons for this.

From the West Indies as a base the explorers went out to the mainland. Consequently, Mexico, Central America, Florida, and the Gulf Coastal Plain were studied, an effort being made to learn something of their past from the early Spaniards to the present time. What nature gave, and what man has done, were the main topics of discussion.

Since the explorations extended north from Mexico and along the Pacific Coast, it was considered best to study California next. So far in their reading and discussion history has received the greater emphasis.

In today's lesson, the geography of California is being considered from a new angle. It was decided to have certain groups report on the products of particular natural regions. From these reports, it is hoped that the children will observe that California has a great variety of products, and that they will be interested to ask the reasons for this. Through discussion it will be learned that this remarkable variety of products is dependent in part upon the various factors of climate: namely, latitude, altitude, nearness to the sea, winds, rainfall, and temperature. Time permitting, the influence of the soil, which differs greatly according to its origin, will be talked about.

LESSON 6. ARITHMETIC

GRADE 4

Review of Zeros Involved in the Four Fundamental Processes

Objective: To gain the correct concept of zero in practical situations. Types of examples will include addition, subtraction, multiplication and short division.

Pupils will be impressed with the following facts to remember about the zero:

Zero (o) means "not any" or "nothing."

o added to a number does not change the number.

o and a number equals the number added.

Zero times any number is zero (o).

Any number times zero equals zero (o).

Zero divided by any number equals zerq (o).

LESSON 7. ENGLISH

GRADE 4

Measuring Pupils' Reading Comprehension

Objective: To measure the pupils' reading comprehension by means of one of the lessons in "Standard Test Lessons in Reading" Book Three by McCall and Crabbs (89-1925) which is a timed objective measure showing the reading grade-score attained by each pupil. Pupils will correct their papers by following the instructions of the teacher who will call upon various pupils for their answers to the test questions pertaining to what they have read. A few pupils may have time for reading prepared selections from books after the test lessons are corrected.

LESSON 8. SOCIAL STUDIES

GRADE 6

Concept of How Geography of British Isles
Affects Their World Relations

Objective: To develop the concept of how the geography of the British Isles has helped Great Britain to take a leading place in the civilized world. "The sixth grade advances beyond the study of separate human-use regions into the study of country personalities. . . . Geographic personality of a country may be defined as a generalization of human activities in relation to natural environment, so stated that it is distinctly individual to that country and cannot be applied to any other country." Quoted by permission of the Society for the Study of Education, 32nd Yearbook, Section IV, pages 261-262 [90 : 1933]. Topics being studied by the pupils include:

Geographic Controls

Variety of Names

Invasions of Several Peoples

Natural Resources
  Physical Characteristics
  Mineral Resources
Industrial Growth
Centers of Educational Interest

LESSON 9. ARITHMETIC

GRADE 5

Practice in Solving Problems Related to Pupils' Interests

Objective: To provide additional meaning to textbook problems by associating units of work with the chief interests and practical experiences of individual pupils. A review of the textbook problems showed that there was ample material for units on camping, gardening, marketing, and sports. Each pupil has chosen one of these units for his particular work. Original problems will also be composed. Groups of pupils will give oral reports concerning their progress. Problems involve applications of whole numbers and fractions.

LESSON 10. ENGLISH

GRADE 4

Use of Dramatization to Promote Desirable Skills and Habits for Speaker and for Audience

Objective: To use dramatization by pupils for the purpose of promoting desirable skills and habits both as speakers and as members of an audience. Included in the specific training is the development of self-confidence and voice-control on the part of the speakers, and of appreciation and courtesy on the part of the audience. The situation also affords opportunity for training in correct English usage. By integrating history with such English activity, the living conditions of the past become more meaningful to the pupils.

Stenographic Records of the Ten Observed Lessons

NOTE: The title preceding each lesson's stenographic report is an abbreviated general objective of the lesson. No mention of these was made except to observers of Group IV, who received copies of the teacher's objectives.

LESSON 1. ENGLISH

GRADE 5

Learning to Write Through Reading

TEACHER: In looking over our stories for today, I find we have several dog stories. We'll start with one of them. Catherine.

CATHERINE: "Bob and his Dog." Plot—To show how truth can make a boy courageous. Incidents—

    A. Bob and his dog walking.

    B. Bob meets Gerald.

    C. Gerald hits and teases dog and Bob tries to stop him. Gerald hits Bob and his dog bites Gerald.

    D. Gerald tells mother and father.

    E. Boy's mother and father are going to have dog shot.

    F. Bob begs them not to shoot the dog.

Characters—Bob, his dog, Gerald, Gerald's mother, Gerald's father.

Time—In the afternoon.

Place—In the woods.

Story—One day as Bob and his dog were walking through the woods they met a boy named Gerald. Gerald hit and teased the dog. When Bob tried to stop him, Gerald hit him, too. By this time the dog was so angry that he bit Gerald. Gerald went home and told his mother and father that Bob's dog had bitten him for no reason at all. The mother said, "He must be a vicious dog. We shall have him shot." His father agreed to this. Bob heard about this and went to the boy's mother and father begging them not to have his dog shot. He tried to explain but they would not listen. Finally the father said, "All right, we will listen." Bob said, "My dog would not have bitten your boy if he had not teased and hit him. I tried to stop Gerald but he hit me. My dog thought that I was hurt and just gave him a little bite on his arm." "But," said the mother "when he came home he had teeth marks on his arm." "Maybe he did it with his own teeth," said Bob. "He told us that he did not do anything to the dog," said the father. "Oh, he is lying to you!" exclaimed Bob angrily. "Please do not have my dog shot." "We will see if you are telling the truth," said Gerald's father sternly. He called Gerald. The boy came down. When he saw Bob he told his father that he had lied and that he wouldn't do it again. Bob went home very happy. Gerald's father remarked as Bob went out of sight, "There goes a manly boy, Gerald. I wish you would try to be more like him."

TEACHER: Before we criticize Catherine's story, let someone tell us in what order we give our criticisms.

DONALD: What we're going to do to make the story better.

LUCY: Good things.

TEACHER: And next?

ARTHUR: Bad things.

TEACHER: Things not so good. They may not always be bad.

NANCY: Shouldn't we tell why things are good or bad?

TEACHER: Yes.

JULIA: Suggestions for improvement.

TEACHER: Yes, let us hear some good things about Catherine's story. Are the introduction and the incidents good? Let us see how well we can do this.

JULIA: I think the plot is good.

DONALD: I should think you would tell why the boy was brave.

TEACHER: How does her plot show that?

EARL: It tells where the boy went and tried to show what Gerald did.

TEACHER: Who is the brave boy?

JIM: Bob.

TEACHER: And what makes him so brave?

RICHARD: Because he wanted to save the dog.

TEACHER: How did he show his bravery?

PERRY: Because he knew that he was right.

DONALD: Miss ———, it showed that he didn't give up because he loved his dog so much.

TEACHER: Have you further suggestions and comments on Catherine's story?

JULIA: I think she had too many Gerald's and Bob's.

CATHERINE: I guess I did.

TEACHER: Catherine worked quite hard to get the Gerald's and Bobs straightened out. I think you'll find that she has handled that quite nicely. Any other suggestions? What did she do in her introduction?

NANCY: She told the time and place.

TEACHER: Did she use an incident to introduce her characters or did she simply introduce them to us by giving the time and place in one sentence?

DONALD: She introduced them near the beginning.

TEACHER: Where did you meet the boys?

WILLIAM: In the first sentence.

TEACHER: Read your first sentence, Catherine.

CATHERINE: "One day when Bob and his dog were walking through the woods they met a boy named Gerald."

TEACHER: Has anyone else a suggestion? They apparently liked your story, Catherine. Let's hear Donald's story.

DONALD: (Reads story) "Camping Fun"

Plot—To show what fun you can have when you go hunting.

Time—Present.

Place—On an old farm.

Characters—Father, Tom and Junior.

Story—On a little old farm near the edge of a wood there lived a boy named Tom. Tom was a boy who liked to hunt. One day Tom asked his father if he could go hunting. "You may, but take care of yourself," said father. "Yes," replied Tom, full of joy as he ran over to get his friend Junior to go, too. "I don't know if I can, but I'll ask Maw," said Junior. "Well, hurry up," called Tom. Soon Junior came running over with his answer. "Hey, Tom," shouted Junior, "Maw said I could go." "That's fine," said Tom. "I'll meet you around six o'clock in the morning. Get all your things packed." Both boys ran home. The next morning everything was set to go. The boys started off on their long journey. When they had walked a long time they grew hungry. "Hey, Tom, let's stop and have a bite to eat," called Junior. "Okay," replied Tom. While they were eating Tom suddenly shouted out, "A snake!" "You're hearing things," said Junior busily eating. "I guess you're right," responded Tom. Soon they were finished eating. When they got up Tom's sharp eye saw a snake just ready to bite Junior. Tom hollered out, "Watch out, Junior." Junior turned around to see what the matter was. When he saw the snake he ran just in the nick of time to get out of its way. Tom killed the snake with a big club. They went on until they saw a flock of wild ducks. Bang, Bang, went their rifles and down came two ducks. "I got a nice one," said Tom. "Me, too," shouted Junior. "Let's try and get some more, and then go home," said Junior. "All right," agreed Tom. When it was dark each boy had five ducks. "I think we better camp here for the night. It's getting too late to go home," replied

Tom. "We can make a pine tent." After working several hours they finished the tent. They gathered plenty of wood for a fire. They built the fire to keep animals away. At night the fire went out. A large grizzly bear entered the tent. It looked curiously around. Soon he spotted Tom and Junior. Junior began to feel cold and woke up. When he saw the bear he woke up Tom. They grabbed their rifles quickly and shot at the bear. They watched the bear drop to the ground. The next morning they went home and gave their mothers the ducks. The bear skin was made into two rugs for souvenirs.

DONALD: Any comments or questions?

NANCY: In some places you could have left out Tom's and Bob's names. I can't tell you just where because the story was so long.

CATHERINE: In the sentence where you said he asked the mother if he could go and then he came back and said, "Yep" you should have said "Yes."

DONALD: These boys are not educated boys.

TEACHER: Donald is using the language he thinks boys like these would use.

JULIA: His plot shows how much fun boys can have in the woods.

WILLIAM: His plot shows that camping is great fun.

TEACHER: That was the same thing that Julia said.

LUCY: I don't think they should have shot the birds.

TEACHER: That was because they wanted something to eat. Donald is a hunter. He thinks it's all right.

CATHERINE: I liked it when Junior woke up and saw the bear.

WILLIAM: I think one part of the plot showed sportsmanship.

TEACHER: It is probable there was sportsmanship shown.

DONALD: You don't have to be a sport just because you get a grizzly bear.

TEACHER: What was the climax of the story?

EARL: When the boys woke up and saw the bear.

TEACHER: You might say the climax would be a little later than that.

CATHERINE: I was going to say the same thing.

WILLIAM: I think it was when the boys went home.

MURIEL: I think the climax would be where they shot the bear.

TEACHER: That's what I thought.

EARL: I don't know how they could get away from the snake so fast.

DONALD: It takes longer when you write it, but if you were saying it it would be quicker. I couldn't find any faster words.

TEACHER: When the boy was rescued from the snake, what expression did Donald use?

EARL: He said that the boy ran away quickly.

WILLIAM: He said he got away just "in the nick of time."

TEACHER: How many incidents did Donald have?

EARL: About six incidents.

TEACHER: Name the first incident.

PUPIL: Where he asked his father.

WARREN: Making arrangements with Junior.

ARTHUR: Going to the woods.

PERRY: Where they shot the ducks.

JULIA: Where they ate their lunch.

TEACHER: That came before the duck-shooting.

PERRY: When they made camp.

TEACHER: How many parts were there to the conclusion?

CHARLES: Two parts.

TEACHER: You see that we may have more than one part in the conclusion.

CATHERINE: When arriving home, taking the ducks to the mother, and making the bear skins into rugs.

JULIA: "Friendliness Repaid"—report.

Plot—To show that kindness to animals will bring happiness.

Introduction—Time—Once upon a time.

Place—In the step-mother's house.

Characters—Step-mother, Step-daughter, stray dog, Farmer, Farmer's Wife.

Body—

A. In the woods.

B. Lost in the woods.

C. Dog saves her.

Conclusion—Gets a good home.

Story—Once upon a time there lived a mean old step-mother with a lovely step-daughter. She did not feed the girl very much. One day the step-mother told her to go out in the woods and chop wood for the fire. Soon after breakfast the girl set out with some food she had saved for her lunch. While she was there she heard a bark. A big ugly dog stood near her. Since she knew the dog must be hungry she gave him some food. He licked her hand as if to say, "Thank you," and disappeared. On the way home the girl got lost in the woods. It was growing dark. She stumbled along trying to find her way home. Suddenly she felt herself sinking into water. She heard the patter of feet coming toward her. A dark shaggy form rushed to her rescue. In a moment the dog held her firmly by her dress. It was the very dog she had befriended that morning. He barked and barked and dragged her safely to shore. He barked again and again louder and louder until he woke a farmer near by. The farmer came out with a lantern and took the girl and the dog in the house where his good wife warmed, fed them, and put the girl to bed. The next morning the girl told the farmer and his wife everything that had happened. They took the girl and the dog into their home where they lived happily ever after. As for the step-mother, she fell in the well and got drowned.

DONALD: I think that you told the plot in the title.

TEACHER: What do you think the plot is?

JULIA: To show that kindness to another should bring happiness.

DONALD: I think that the plot should be about the step-mother. I think that the step-mother is more important than the dog.

TEACHER: Julia perhaps had two plots. The story should be a lesson to step-mothers, and boys and girls too.

EARL: I think the story was well written. I think there were a few ideas from stories which we have read.

TEACHER. What books have we read that make you think of Julia's story?

PAUL: Reddy Ringlets.

MARVIN: The Tinder Box.

ANTONE: The Soldier's Reprieve.

TEACHER: Another one?

VERA: Ishmael.

TEACHER: Yes, "Ishmael" story of the stray dog. Julia didn't really take any one person's ideas. She combined several ideas from different stories.

LESSON 2. SOCIAL STUDIES

GRADE 4

Introducing a Desert Country

TEACHER: What is one type of region we discussed this term?

EDWARD: Cold region.

TEACHER: Will you show us a place on the map that represents that type of region.

MAY: Antarctica. (Locates it on wall map of world.)

TEACHER: We also talked about the land in this region. (Indicates northeastern section of South America on wall map of world.)

DOROTHY: A part of South America.

TEACHER: What part?

DOROTHY: Brazil.

GLADYS: Amazon Basin or Valley.

TEACHER: What is this line? (Traces equator.)

ROGER: Equator.

TEACHER: So we know the area has a certain climate, Virginia?

VIRGINIA: Hot.

TEACHER: We also find it to be a wet region. Let us think of another type of region. What is the particular one I am pointing to now? Does anyone know the name of this country?

PATRICK: Arabia.

TEACHER: Does anyone know anything about Arabia through reading, or from the movies or the radio?

NORMAN: It is a desert country.

TEACHER: That's right Norman, how did you know that?

NORMAN: I read it in a book.

TEACHER: What do you know about the land?

PATRICK: It is a very dry region.

TEACHER: That's very true; we're going to find in our reading that it is a dry region.

RUTH: In a desert, there isn't very much water and the people would naturally have to go a long way without water.

TEACHER: Did you notice any pictures placed around the room that would give you an idea of the desert? (Pauses while pupils look at large pictures of desert scenes.) As I trace my finger around Arabia what do you notice about its position? Edward?

EDWARD: It looks like a boot.

TEACHER: Yes, it has somewhat the shape of a boot.

NORMAN: It looks like a flashlight.

TEACHER: What's this all around here? (Traces the coastline.)

MAY: There is water around three sides.

TEACHER: Do you know the name given to such a piece of land as this?

HELEN: Peninsula.

TEACHER: Yes, Arabia is a large peninsula. This is one of the words in our new vocabulary list. (Points to word on blackboard.) That comes from a word meaning "almost an island." How would you travel to Arabia from our country? May, would you like to come up and show us?

MAY: (Goes up to map) Start from New York.

TEACHER: How would you travel?

MAY: By boat.

TEACHER: Across what?

MAY: Atlantic ocean.

TEACHER: Do you know what this particular narrow passageway is?

GLADYS: Red Sea.

TEACHER: The Strait of Gibraltar leads into what body of water?

MAY: The Red Sea.

TEACHER: Can you hear her, Terry?

TERRY: The Mediterranean Sea!

TEACHER: And then there is another narrow passageway here that you pass through to get to the Red Sea.

PATRICK: It is a canal. Suez Canal to the Red Sea.

TEACHER: We probably dock at a place right here. I'm pointing now to a town called Jedda. There are not many docks along the coast of Arabia. Can you tell why?

JOSEPH: It is a desert land.

TEACHER: Most all of Arabia is a desert so that it would mean that water would be hard to obtain, and not a place where people would be apt to settle. Let's think more about the type of country itself. So far we have mentioned that it is a dry area.

RUTH: It would be sandy.

TEACHER: It would be sandy because it is dry. What kind of land is very sandy and dry, Tillie?

TILLIE: A desert is sandy and dry.

TEACHER: The equator runs through part of South America. Arabia is farther away from the equator but it is still near enough to be warm all through the year. Part of the year it is very hot in Arabia. Is there anything else that you would think of that should be mentioned about the type of country? The northeast trade winds blow across Arabia. These winds come from a land area. What effect would that have upon Arabia?

VIRGINIA: They would be dry winds.

TEACHER: Coming from the land they wouldn't have an opportunity to get water. Knowing that this is a hot dry country what type of homes would you expect to find? You'll find out by reading later, but let's think about it a few minutes.

GLADYS: Tents.

TEACHER: Do you see anything around the room that might give you an idea of how they live?

ROBERT: The picture right over there.

TEACHER: Yes, this happens to be a scene in a town. There are not many towns because most of Arabia is a desert. We don't expect to see many types of buildings. Do they look like our homes?

NORMAN: They look like square boxes on top of each other.

TEACHER: Do you notice anything else that makes them very different from ours? It is very true they are built on terraces. George?

GEORGE: The trees are different.

TEACHER: What kind of trees are they?

GEORGE: Palm trees.

TEACHER: Yes, they grow in tropical areas. In which climatic belt on the earth's surface does Arabia lie? Could you come up and place Arabia here? (Referring to climatic belts on board map.)

JOSEPH: Tropic of Cancer.

TEACHER: The Tropic of Cancer passes through Arabia and that is the type of region where these trees grow. Does anyone notice the roofs of the houses?

RUTH: They are flat roofs.

TEACHER: Why don't we have flat roofs?'

RUTH: Because ours are made of shingles.

TEACHER: These homes are made of brick baked in the sun. Why don't they build them of wood? Some of the other pupils that haven't spoken yet may tell us why Arabians do not build these homes of wood?

OLGA: Because it's very hot and brick is cooler.

TEACHER: Yes, are there other reasons?

VIRGINIA: Because it would rot.

NORMAN: Because they can't get it.

TEACHER: There are no trees with which to build homes.

JOSEPH: Mostly palm trees that are scarce.

TEACHER: The trees are so scarce that they use mud baked into bricks. We still haven't found out why they have flat roofs.

EDWARD: The people have ladders to go up to the second floor.

TEACHER: Did you read that?

EDWARD: I saw a picture of it.

TEACHER: I didn't know that.

TERRY: They don't get much rain.

TEACHER: Good for you Terry. Why don't we have our roofs flat?

TERRY: So the rain will run off.

TEACHER: To permit the rain to run off the roof. Do Arabian people have to make provision for that?

NORMAN: No, Miss ——.

TEACHER: There is little rain to run off so they can build flat roofs. Not all of the people in Arabia live in this type of home. What do we call people who live in Arabia?

ROGER: Arabs.

TEACHER: There are different kinds of Arabs. Do the people who live in the desert parts of Arabia have a special name?

GEORGE: Arabians.

TEACHER: All the people who live in Arabia are called Arabians. The people who live in the desert are called Bedouins, and the Bedouins are called nomads. Does anyone know the meaning of nomads? Minette, will you look up the meaning of nomads in the dictionary? Certain people who live in Arabia live in deserts. Would they live in homes like this, do you expect? Emma?

EMMA: No, Miss ——.

TEACHER: How do you think they live?

GUSTAVE: They have tents.

TEACHER: Why do those people live in tents?

EMMA: The land is too dry to make houses.

JOSEPH: They have no water.

TEACHER: When they have no more water they pack up and move somewhere else.

JOSEPH: Because they need water.

TEACHER: When the cattle have exhausted the supply of grass they go on to another place.

RUTH: Bedouins live in the very hottest part of Arabia.

TEACHER: You will learn more about the homes of the people as you read. We'll think a little now about the food. What do you expect to learn about the foods? Would the people have a great variety of foods?

HELEN: No, Miss ——.

TEACHER: Why don't they have many kinds of foods?

HELEN: It doesn't rain there very often and nothing grows.

MINETTE: (Reads definition of nomads.)

TEACHER: Then what people in Arabia are nomads?

PATRICK: Bedouins.

TEACHER: Yes, they wander from place to place. Perhaps we'll find out more about foods through reading. They probably don't have many kinds of foods because they can't raise them. Would you know of any kind that they do raise?

MAY: Fruits.

TEACHER: What kind of fruits?

ROBERT: Dates.

TEACHER: How did you know about that?

ROBERT: I read it in a book.

TEACHER: That's fine, that's going to be a help to you. What is another type of food that people in Arabia have?

JOSEPH: Coconuts.

TEACHER: Do coconuts grow in Arabia, Joseph? If you come across such information will you let us know.

ROBERT: Water is near trees.

TEACHER: That also works the other way around. Trees need water to grow. Do you see any pictures that give you an idea about the kind of clothing these people wear?

OLGA: There is a picture that shows the kind of clothing. (Points to wall pictures.)

EMMA: It looks very light.

TEACHER: Yes, light clothing because it is so hot. Something else?

MARY: They wear clothing that practically covers them.

TEACHER: Why do you think that they wear this type of clothing?

ROBERT: To protect them from the heat.

TEACHER: To protect their bodies from the sun. What else?

NORMAN: To protect them from sand storms.

TEACHER: What were you going to say?

PATRICK: I was going to say what Norman said.

TEACHER: Doesn't the clothing look loose, or does it seem to fit to them tightly?

GLADYS: Loose.

TEACHER: That is one feature of the clothing of the people in Arabia, they wear loose clothing. Why do they wear loose clothing?

EDWARD: Because it's cooler.

MAY: They wear hoods around their heads.

TEACHER: They do wear cloths around their heads, and it goes down over their shoulders. This comes in very nicely when they have sand storms.

JOSEPH: They cover their faces with it.

TEACHER: It protects their eyes and noses from the sand which blows.

TILLIE: I know they use the cloth to protect their heads from the sun.

TEACHER: Yes, it protects them from the sun and sand storms. What are the means of land travel?

SALLY: Camels.

TEACHER: Yes. Why are camels such a helpful means of travel in hot dry countries?

GEORGE: Camels can go many days without water.

TEACHER: Yes. They only need water twice a week. What is there about the camel's feet that is very helpful?

EDWARD: I don't know.

(Teacher shows picture of camel.)

EDWARD: The hump in the camel's back is fat.

TEACHER: What is there about the camel's feet that adapt him to desert travel?

TILLIE: They can walk through the sand because they are so thin.

TEACHER: I don't think they are so thin.

GUSTAVE: They are long.

TEACHER: Something about their feet makes it easy for the camel to travel over the sand without sinking in.

MAY: They have cuts in their feet. (Discussion follows as to just what she means by cuts in their feet.)

TEACHER: Humps on the back is another reason the camel is useful. They can use them for carrying baggage.

MAY: They also carry packages in carts.

TEACHER: Did you read that, I thought they used camel's backs.

MAY: Yes, I read that.

JOSEPH: That's part of the saddle that's used on the camel.

TEACHER: Some of you may want to read about their ways of making a living. As I call a group you will please select books and go back to your chairs to find a topic you are interested in studying. To what part of the book will you turn to find the topic?

ROGER: Index.

TEACHER: That's one part.

ROGER: Table of contents.

TEACHER: In what continent is Arabia?

TERRY: Asia.

TEACHER: Arabia is one of the countries that makes up the continent of Asia. Group one may select books from the reference table. I am also selecting one member of each group to choose a topic for the group. Group two may select books for a special report. Group three. Joseph, will you select a topic from the board? (Groups 4, 5, and 6 select books after group leaders are selected.) Select your topics from the board to read about in the books. Mary, would group six be willing to read about the "Characteristics of the Region"? That's the one that's left.

MARY: Yes, Miss ———.

TEACHER: We won't have time to read about our topics here, so bring your books with you when you leave. Keep them for reading upstairs. Notice I have also given you some suggestions on the board for library reading.

TOPICS OF INTEREST

I. Characteristics of Region (Group 6)
II. Types of Shelter (homes) (Group 1)
III. Commonly Used Foods (Group 4)
IV. Kinds of Dress (clothing) (Group 2)
V. Means of Land Travel (Group 3)
VI. Ways of Making a Living (Group 5)

VOCABULARY
(ON BOARD)

peninsular	caravan
Arabs	oasis
Bedouins	irrigation
nomads	

(One person from each group selected a topic for that group and placed his group number on the board next to the topic selected.)

LESSON 3. ARITHMETIC

GRADE 4

Drill of Fundamental Number Facts

TEACHER: Boys and girls, I have placed on the board some points which you must observe carefully when you are doing your arithmetic. On papers, as I have been correcting them, I have found all these points which must be observed carefully in order to solve your problems correctly. Some of these are not correct. We shall find the mistake.

Multiply	Add	Subtract			
0 5	0 5	5 9232			
5 0	5 0	0 896	8	2	9
0 0	5 5	5 9336	42)3497	21)5678	64)5696

Multiply			
847	3	6	
362	34)1428	88)5997	
1694		528	
5082		71	88 64
2541			7 9
306614			616 576

TEACHER: Will you read the first examples, Frank?

FRANK: $5 \times 0 = 0$, $0 \times 5 = 0$.

TEACHER: You see this number tells us just how many times this number is multiplied by it. Now you have to look and see what the first word is—in this case, multiply.

CLARICE: Add, 5 plus 0 is 5, 0 plus 5 is 5.

TEACHER: What does it say here? (Points to example on board.)

ELIZABETH: Subtract, $5 - 0 = 5$.

TEACHER: The next one, can someone tell me what is wrong with this example?

EDWARD: It says subtract 9 into 12.

TEACHER: Why do you say into 12?

EDWARD: 9 into 12 is.

TEACHER: Now, just wait a minute, do the whole example.

EDWARD: 6 from 12 is 6; 10 from 13 is 3; 9 from 12 is 3; and 1 from 9, that should be 8.

TEACHER: Yes, we'll erase that and put 8. Because you increased the 2 to 12, you place a 1 under the 9. Now we'll read this example in multiplication. You have three figures. Multiply the first one, then multiply by the figure in the second place and put that over two spaces, then multiply by the figure in the third place and put it over three places. What is one thing we must always remember when we do this example?

CLARICE: To put the figures right under the number we are multiply-ing by.

TEACHER: We'll do this example in division. What is the trouble with this?

SARAH: The 8 should be over the 9.

TEACHER: Why should the 8 be over the 9?

SARAH: Because 42 can't go into 34.

TEACHER: 34 is too small, so what do I have to do?

SARAH: Put it over the third number.

TEACHER: Now I have this in the third place. Is that right?

HARRIET: Yes.

TEACHER: Here I have it in the second place, and you say it is right. (Points to third division example.)

ANN: Yes.

TEACHER: What is the trouble with this example?

CLARICE: 9 times 64 is 576 and 576 is larger than 569 so you must take the next smaller number. When she was doing this example she said 6 into 56 is contained 9 times.

TEACHER: Isn't 6 contained in 56 9 times?

CLARICE: She should multiply and then compare.

TEACHER: If we did that we should find that this number is larger than this. Look at this and find out what is the trouble.

LILLY: Four times. She put three up in the quotient.

TEACHER: What would tell us it is wrong?

LILLY: After she has subtracted, the answer will be larger than the divisor.

TEACHER: What would be a better word than "answer"?

LILLY: Remainder.

TEACHER: If she had compared she would have found that the number was larger than the figure she had divided by. What should she do?

CLARICE: Study her tables.

TEACHER: (Next example.) Can you explain this, Ann?

ANN: (No response.)

TEACHER: Is it right?

FRANK: No.

TEACHER: What is wrong with it?

FRANK: She should have multiplied 6 by 88.

TEACHER: Look where she put this seven. Why did she multiply that by 7, Elizabeth?

ELIZABETH: Because when she multiplied it, 8 into 59 goes 7 times.

TEACHER: There are seven 8's in 59. She did just right, but she didn't put it down. When she compared, what did she find, Elizabeth?

ELIZABETH: That 616 is larger than 599.

TEACHER: So what did she do?

ELIZABETH: She took the next number smaller than that.

TEACHER: And then compared, is that right?

ELIZABETH: Yes.

Boys and girls whose names are on the board may take their places. If you need any material from the table you may go and get it. Those who are using cards in the group may go to their places. All others may open their workbooks and go to work. (Teacher goes among children giving individual suggestions and comments.)

TEACHER: I hear some pieces of chalk making a rasping noise. If you tip the chalk a little it won't make that noise. Hold it this way. It will soon wear off.

Children at board: Arlene, Elizabeth, Ann, Grace, Louis, Harriet, Beatrice, Peter and Samuel.

Three children work in a group at front of room: Margaret, Peg, and Nicky.

The other children work individually or in pairs or groups either at the board or at their desks.

(Remarks made by teacher to individuals or groups as she examines the work going on.)

How many 2's are there in nine?

There is a mistake in your work, call me when you find it.

You forgot to put the dollar sign there.

Where should the decimal point be?

Check your work again and call me when you find your mistake.

That's right.

You are on page 73? Splendid, that's fine.

You don't need to put your decimal points there.

Oh, yes, you had to find a mistake on this. That's right, fine.

There's your mistake.

TEACHER: Close your books, boys and girls. Those at the board put the material on this table. Place your workbooks on the little shelves under your chairs. (Teacher distributes diagnostic multiplication sheets.) This morning we shall have a check-up on multiplication. Now if you find that you failed on any of the tables, say the 8th, what are you going to do about it?

EDWARD: Study the 8th table.

TEACHER: And if you failed on the 7th table?

PETER: Study the 7th table.

TEACHER: Write your name on the line where it says "Name." Take your pencils. Just another second or two. Begin. (Teacher times them.) Pupils turn over their papers and put their pencils down when through.

TEACHER: Stop. The children at the back of the room bring forward the papers, please. Peg, collect the papers. Thank you. Take from under your chairs the workbooks. Take the pencils and erasers with you. Class excused.

LESSON 4. ENGLISH

GRADE 6

Formulating Standards for Written Expression

TEACHER: Boys and girls: So that we can hear from every group this morning, we are going to have only the reports read and no group discussions. Take some mental notes and next time, we shall discuss what you like about each report and how it can be made better.

Group 1. SUSAN: The chief value of a narration or a story is to give pleasure. We try in our narrations to have an interesting plot. We think out our first sentence to interest at once by a startling leader. We include rich vocabulary. When we appeal to the senses—sight, sound, touch, smell, and taste, it makes our narration more interesting. Also, dialogue helps interest. We think out our last sentence so that it causes a smile, causes a regret, or creates a desire to hear more. I will read my narration: "A Surprise for the Twins." The outline includes:

    I. Orphelia and Marcus have a surprise
    II. The ride through the park
    III. Home again

Orphelia and Marcus were twins who lived in Rome. Their father was in Greece on a business trip. They were left in the care of their mother. One day, when Orphelia was reading a story and was just reaching the climax of it, someone knocked at the door. She was so startled that she jumped up. The book fell on the floor. By the time she had picked it up, Marcus cried, "Mother, mother. A letter for you!" Mother came into the room, flopped down in a chair, and took the letter. This is what it read: Orgas Way, Rome, Italy, April 5. 1937, Dear Maria, This is my week of vacation. I would like to take the twins to the country. I will call for them tomorrow at sunrise. I hope they will have a nice time. I have a surprise for them, too. Lovingly, Your Sister. Orphelia and Marcus were on their way at last. It was really wonderful to see the sunrise. The sky seemed to be every color of the rainbow. You would have loved to see the smiling faces of them all as they moved swiftly and smoothly on the wonderfully built roads in their aunt's carriage. On and on they sped in and out of the winding roads, up hill and down hill, and on many roads. They were riding through the park when suddenly,— why what do you suppose happened? A flea had just bitten one of the horses. He began to gallop frantically. Of course all the other horses had to run, too. Toward sunset their aunt took them home. What a surprise was awaiting them there! As soon as they passed the threshold, their eyes caught a glimpse of something. Do you know what it was? No, I guess I'll have to tell you. It was their own father. He had returned from Greece at about noontime. The twin's aunt stayed with them all the rest of the week, much to their joy. If you would like to know what happened the next few days, all you have to do is to ask Orphelia and Marcus about it.

Group 2. PETER: When our group wrote our description in the class-room we pretended we were artists and painted pictures on imaginary canvas. We tried to make sure our fine senses were alert and to tell all details clearly and vividly. Taking a point of view and holding to it is very important. I will read my description. Do you notice I haven't made a title for this but I'll ask for suggestions from you in the next lesson?

The sun is now descending and nightfall draws near. In a short time the moon like a boat will drift across the sky which is like a sea. The stars like little tug boats draw the large liner. But soon an enormous cloud covers the large liner. It is just like a smoke screen. Then the stars put on their lights so bright that you cannot see them. They then go into action. The liner puts on its lights, too. It looks like a great ball of fire. The stars seem to grasp the cloud and pull it away. The sky is now clear and the liner now continues its voyage. The beams from the liner seem to dance because of the victory. When the large liner comes to the middle of the sea, it seems to dock for a while. But soon it starts on its journey again. Then the tug boats dim their lights and the boat dims its lights. This goes on and on, but some times the tug boats and liner do not win the fight and it is dark.

Group 3. MICHAEL (chairman of letter-writing group): In our friendly letters we try to begin promptly and interestingly. We write in conversational style, that is, we write as though we were actually talking to the person. It is interesting to ask questions and answer them and bring back the past and plan the future. It is a good plan to make such an ending as will invite an answer. William will read his friendly letter. Hotel Roma, Rome, Italy, April 1, 1937. Dear Frank, I arrived here in Italy last Tuesday on the Rex. The boat docked at Genoa and from there I took the train to Rome, a trip which was very interesting. I really could tell you more about it but haven't time for that now. You will hear more about it in another letter from me. A friend and I visited St. Peter's Church yesterday and looked at almost everything. We saw the large statue of St. Peter which is about seventy-five feet high. We also saw the works of many famous sculptors in one of the long corridors and looked at the paintings on the ceiling of the church done by Michael Angelo. Some are still unfinished. Today, I have planned to go on an over-night motor trip to Naples and Pompeii to see the ruins of the city which was buried by lava in 79 A.D. In the museum at Naples, there are people cast with lava; this kept them for so many years. They look something like Egyptian mummies. Oh! and I want to tell you that I have the stamps you wanted, twenty-five in all. I will take them back with me in about four weeks. How was the Easter holiday in America? It was very solemn here. Although there is much to see here, I miss hearing from my friends. The driver of the automobile has been waiting for quite a while, I'm afraid he will be loosing his patience.

Affectionately yours, William.

TEACHER: William, pronounce "solemn."

WILLIAM: Solemn.

Group 4. GRACE (chairman of biography group): In writing a biography, choose a person of some special interest to you. In the sixth grade we limit the biography to three paragraphs. In the first, tell necessary statistics; in the second tell some instance worth remembering; in the last paragraph state clearly the person's gift. Mary will read the biography for our group.

MARY: Wolfgang Mozart. I—Statistics. II—Mozart plays his first piece. III—A genius.

On January 27, 1756, Wolfgang Mozart was born in Salzburg, Austria. His death occurred in 1791 when he was only about thirty-five years old. His father was Vice-Master in the Bishop's Chapel and a fine musician, besides. Mozart's father would give music lessons to his daughter, Marianne, who was five years older than Wolfgang. One day, Mozart asked his father, who had just taught Marianne a new piece, to teach him how to play the harpsichord. His parents claimed his fingers were too small and weak to play. After supper that night, Mozart slipped away unnoticed. A few minutes later the piece Marianne had learned that day was being played beautifully. Mozart's father thought Marianne was playing it but she came before him while the music kept on. Mystified, they went to the music room and there was Mozart playing on the harpsichord! Mozart begged his father to teach him and he agreed. He was only three years old at that time. Mozart composed many compositions now famous. At the tender age of five, he began composing minuets that would take a very experienced musician to write. There is no doubt that Wolfgang Mozart was a genius.

TEACHER: Next group.

Group 5. LOUISE: Exposition is really explaining something. You may explain many things such as how to make something, or how to play a game. It is necessary to clearly organize what you are going to say, then say it with enthusiasm. I will read my exposition. "A Good Dinnertime Game."

At dinner after everyone is seated, you would probably hear something like this: "Where is the Forfeit Box?" Then someone would get up and get it. Then the game starts. The conversation begins. We talk along for a while and perhaps someone says, "Nope" and is forefeited a cent. We can't say penny for there is no such thing in common use in American money. Here are some common errors that are frequently made by everyone. After them are their forfeit prices: Okay—1¢, Uh-huh—1¢, Nope—1¢, Huh—1¢, Ain't—1¢, Yeah—1 1¢, Goin'—1¢, Comin'—1¢, 'Scuse—1¢, Penny—1¢, etc. All the money from the forfeits is put in a box. We now have approximately five dollars in the box, but the game has improved our language fifty percent. Why don't some of you try this game?

Group 6. ELLEN: The language of verse is usually a marching, or dancing, or tripping kind of language. It is always keeping time to some melody or tune. My poem suggests the river rippling along. The title of my verse is "Evening in the Woods."

> In the woods where all was still,
> I heard the cry of the Whip-o-will,
> And the sound of the brook as it rippled along,
> Never ceasing its cheerful song.
> There in the shade of a tree I stood,
> Cast over me like a great green hood,
> The trees rose to a terrible height,
> Around me stole the darkening night.

ELLEN: Ann will read her verse.

ANN: "The First Persian War."

> The first Persian War,
> Was without law.
> Greece's leader was Miltiades,
> Persia had brave Darius.
> They fought with bow and arrow;
> Shooting through passages narrow.
> Shields and swords were also used,
> Brave Persia was going to lose.

The fight is now ended,
And the Persians fast run
For the news is out;
Greece has now won.

JOHN: The title of my verse is "Sailing."

Sailing, sailing down the bay
To strange lands so far away
Taking cargo and sailor-men
That may never come home again.
Sailing through the ocean wide
While foaming high is the tide
That is hitting the stern so high
And making the ships say good-bye.
Sailing to lands far away
Bringing the news of the day,
Over the ocean and blue sea,
Maybe India or Bengal Bay.

MATTHEW: The title of my verse is "Phidippides."

As I look about the market place
I think I see a familiar face
Who I wonder could that be
I hear a voice say Phidippides.
Is that he who ran so fast
Who ran to Athens to tell the past
The people say he is dead
But there's his image before my head.

DAVID: The title of my verse is "The Norsemen."

The Norsemen roved the seas
Driven by the strong breeze
Sometimes down the Rhine
Bounded by the brine.
In their little boats
Holding on by ropes
Trying to be courageous
Fighting thru all the ages.
Norsemen went to far-off places
Meeting people of different races
They landed in America or U. S. A.
But never left the shattered flag of Norway

TEACHER: In our group discussions upstairs, there were tie votes for the reading to the class of a narration, description, and biography. Since we have a few minutes remaining, we can have the other ones read. I know you are anxious to read them.

SALLY: "The Lame Boy Wins the Quarter."

TEACHER: This is a narration.

SALLY: I—The Plan, II—Value, III—The Discovery, IV—Returned, V—The Winner.

One brilliant afternoon Aunt Gen's distinct voice called, "Children." They came to answer her call in great speed, some from the fields, some from the forests, and from many other places and directions. All seemed very excited with cheeks beaming brightly. Without hesitation Aunt Gen revealed the following plan. Whoever could gather the most berries would receive twenty-five cents which meant a great deal to these children because they did not receive much money for there was scarcely any place to spend it. They were to have them all picked by supper-time. Aunt Gen thought this plan to be a grand one because it would bring the children an appetite for supper and of course the berries could be used for cooking. Soon, excited and pleased with the plan, they ran into the house to get bags or baskets. One came out, then another, and still another and finally they all came out and ran in different directions. Jack, a lame boy of course could not go far from home so he lingered around the edge of the forest. All of a sudden he spotted a nearby berry bush covered with large ripe berries that came off with a mere touch. About supper-time they returned with bags and baskets half-filled, saying, "The berries all seemed to be picked." Standing near the corner Jack spoke up, "There seemed to be an abundance." Aunt Gen came in and looked over the bags and baskets. Soon she came over to Jack's and looked at him in amazement and said, "I told you never to go to such a remote place as the far part of the forest and it seems to me you disobeyed me." "But, Aunt Gen," he interrupted, "I didn't. I found them at the edge of the forest." "Well, Jack wins the quarter," replied Aunt Gen in a delightful manner which made Jack seem proud and happy because this was the first time he had beaten the others.

TEACHER: The second description.

JOHN: "As the Day Passes."

At dawn the sun rises slowly in yonder east with its enormous bright shining colors. The birds and their sweet songs invite you to rise from bed and dance on this beautiful day. The morning is filled with healthful air, and people are busily going to work to start another active day. The morning is passing quickly and it soon becomes noon. Then the loud noises of the whistles and the city is filled with commotion once more. The rumble of cars and the puffing of trains is heard. The noises cease a little now as the working people go busily about their business. All through the morning and afternoon cloud pictures are being painted in the sky. Evening is just around the corner as the sun with its reddish-orange color disappears in the west. Pictures in the sky vanish, also, as the sky turns a dark blue. As the night grows older, the world seems to grow silent.

TEACHER: There was a tie in the biography group too.

GRACE: "Joan of Arc." I—Early Life, II—Chosen to save France, III. A great heroine Joan of Arc was born in the year 1411 and she was only twenty years old when she died. She grew up a healthy child, full of play, in the little French town of Donremy. As a little girl she would dance and sing at the village fairs or under the old fairy tree, an ancient tree on which she and the other children used to hang garlands for the fairies, who in their fancy, came to play under it. Little Joan never learned her letters, for very few girls could read or write in those days. But she became very skillful in spinning and sewing. Occasionally she tended the sheep on the hillside. That is the sort of education any village girl would have. One day, when Joan was about twelve, she was in the garden busy with her needle. A very strange and eventful thing happened. She seemed to hear the Angelus bell ring out from the church steeple and to see a great beam of light fall into the shady gardens; and she believed a divine voice spoke to her. In fear and wonder, she listened to the voice from Heaven. It told her to be unafraid, to be good and wise for she had been chosen of Heaven for a great mission. She was to be the person who would set France free and seat the king on his throne. For four years the voice continued and visions of saints came with them. Their voices were preparing her to give aid to the king. When she was seventeen years of age the voices told her it was time to aid the king. For three years this simple peasant girl had taken her place at the head of an army and she routed the English and crowned the king of France. Then Joan of Arc was taken a prisoner and burned at the stake in 1431. She is a heroine of her country and of the world. She has fascinated the historians who have spent many years trying to find the truth about her to explain how she came to do things she did. She has been declared a saint.

TEACHER: Grace, pronounce "historian."

GRACE: Historian.

TEACHER: Jean, you may read your letter.

JEAN: Dear Helen, Did you see many interesting thing in Florida? While you were going swimming there, we were freezing to death up here. Maybe we both will go to Florida some fine day. I am going to see "Maytime" this afternoon starring Nelson Eddy and Jeannette MacDonald. Did you get any new clothes for Easter? I did not. But you wait and see what nice clothes I have when I come to visit you. I am going to get a coat, pocketbook, gloves and shoes all for spring. Have you still got a lot of paper dolls? I hope so. I am going to bring mine down when I come. I can't wait until I arrive at Washington. I miss you terribly. In school our class is studying about Rome. It is very interesting. We have reached the time Augustus Caesar was ruler. He was the nephew of Julius Caesar. Mother and I plan to be in Washington next Friday night. I have lots more to tell you then. Your cousin, Jean. P.S. Is the organ grinder still there?

TEACHER: Boys and girls, although this was the first time that you have read these compositions to your class, you read distinctly and well. You are excused now.

LESSON 5. SOCIAL STUDIES

GRADE 5

Pupil Reports Concerning Products and Geography of California

TEACHER: This morning we shall give some of our reports. While we are hearing the reports, I should like to have you write down any questions that you would like to ask after the reports have been given, or if you think of something you would like to tell us, write that down, too.

JACK: Northern California. (Points to it on map.)

In Northern California are mineral products and sheep. On the western mountain slopes there are forests.

TEACHER: Can you tell us about the trees?

JACK: The trees are oak, pine, fir, cedar and redwood. The redwood tree is fifty to sixty feet around with no limbs for 150 to 200 feet from the ground. These trees are used for railroad ties because they split so easily and stay in the ground so long without rotting. The most important minerals are gold, silver, coal, lead, and phosphate rock. Sheep are raised in the valleys. California is famous for its lamb.

TEACHER: I saw several people writing down some questions. Julia.

JULIA: Sacramento Valley. (Points to it on map.)

The Great Valley of California is divided up into two parts. To the north is the Sacramento Valley which is named after the Sacramento River that flows through it. On the western slopes of the Sierra Nevada mountains are great Sequoia trees. To the north of the valley are great fields of rice. Tons of vegetables are raised and canned. In the valley on the west are wheat, barley and great quantities of almonds. Oranges, lemons, peaches, pears, and plums are raised on the east side. Before they had the Western Pacific Railway, wheat and barley were the chief products, but the farmers found out that they couldn't sell the wheat and barley as cheaply as the midwestern farmers. They began to raise fruits and vegetables such as onions, celery, asparagus. Now that they have the railroad they send goods right across, and can get large prices for them.

CATHERINE: The San Juaquin Valley is also named for the river that drains it. In the southern part of the valley olives, figs, grapes, and oranges grow. The Spanish Mission fathers planted figs and olive orchards, some of which you can still see. California produces almost all of the olives in the United States. Fresno is one of the raisin capitals of the world. Great quantities of grapes are raised for different uses. Some are made into grape juice and wines, some are shipped fresh, and many are made into raisins.

TEACHER: There are very important things to notice in all of these reports.

ANTHONY: Southwestern California. (Points to it on map.)

Southwestern California around Los Angeles grows many valuable farming products and these products, as in other parts of California, are zoned according to their ability to stand the frost. About all they can grow low down in the valley are beets and wheat. Beets grow under ground and can take the frost better than a lot of other vegetables, and the wheat is a strong grain. A little farther up on the slopes of the mountains, peaches and grapes are grown and farther up come oranges and lemons. The lemons are delicate and they need the warm air. Warm air rises, so the frost won't kill the trees near the top or near the middle of the mountains.

TEACHER: What may be on top of the mountains?

ANTHONY: Snow.

Beans are grown along the western coast and they don't need irrigation, even in the rainless summers. Cauliflower is grown in Southern California and some of the best cabbage and lettuce in the United States is grown there. Some of the best English walnuts come from Southern California. They are mostly grown near Los Angeles and Santa Barbara. Many gallons of oil are taken out of oil wells.

TEACHER: Irene, I think it is your turn.

IRENE: Imperial Valley. (Points to it on map.)

The Imperial Valley is sometimes called the Egypt of America. As in Egypt large quantities of dates are grown there. The cotton grown there is like Egyptian cotton. It has long fibers and is especially good for making automobile tires because it is so strong. Huge fields of alfalfa provide feed for many herds of dairy cows. Oranges, lemons, grapefruit, and green vegetables are raised and shipped to all parts of the United States. There are many bees in this part of California so that honey is an important product. The agricultural products of the Imperial Valley are among the most valuable in the world.

WILLIAM: Death Valley. (Points to it on map.)

The products of Death Valley are salt, borax, soda, platinum, iodine, potash, mercury, silica and diatomite. Diatomite is made up of many little plants covered with a quartz-like substance called silica. Platinum looks like silver or white gold, only it is much more valuable. In the marshes where they get borax, they have to hire Chinamen to work because no white person can stand the heat.

TEACHER: There is something over there on the table which should remind you of something you would see if you went to Death Valley.

WILLIAM: They take the borax out in big teams with ten or twenty mules.

TEACHER: Yes, some of you have probably heard the radio program, Death Valley Days.

LUCY: The Mohave and Colorado Deserts. (Points to them on map.)

Southeastern California is made up almost entirely of the Mohave and Colorado Deserts. The Colorado Desert is the hottest part of the United States but the Mohave Desert is the largest in California. Great stretches of sand dunes are covered with sage brush and bunch grass. In the desert a valuable mineral is found—tungsten. It is used for making fine steel for tools and for electric lights. Other minerals are gold, silver, and cement. Borax was discovered in 1926 in the Mohave Desert.

TEACHER: You said they get cement. You didn't mean that, did you?

LUCY: I got that from the book.

TEACHER: It is clay from which cement is made.

GEORGE: What are railroad ties?

WILLIAM: They are logs that go across to hold steel tracks together.

TEACHER: You have probably seen people walking on them, although it is against the law and very dangerous.

RICHARD: What is phosphate rock?

TEACHER: A rock used in making fertilizer.

BARBARA: What kind of climate do the trees have to have?

LOUISE: Some trees have to have warm climates and some have to have cooler climates.

JULIA: If you mean the Sequoias, California is warm, and since they grow in Southern California they must need a warm climate.

TEACHER: Is a warm climate the only thing that there has to be?

JULIA: Rain.

TEACHER: What must they have besides the rain to make them grow?

ANTHONY: Soil.

TEACHER: They must have these two factors—climate and soil. We shall answer that question better in a few minutes.

JULIA: I have one. (A question.) Where does California send most of its products?

TEACHER: Has anyone found that out?

ANTHONY: I think they send most of their things to Mexico and eastern countries.

TEACHER: That showed very good judgment, Anthony.

LOUISE: I think they send most of their things across the seas.

TEACHER: If you think over the reports that have just been given, you will know where they send some things.

GEORGE: All around the world.

TEACHER: Yes, that is correct.

BARBARA: To the west, I mean to the east, across the United States where we live.

ANTHONY: I should think they would send many products to China and Japan.

TEACHER: Yes, they do.

ANTHONY: What products does California need from other states?

PERRY: Most everything is grown there. They don't need much of anything but spices.

TEACHER: He thinks California could do fairly well by itself. Let us see if we can find out just what she has to have. What does she use a great deal of when she ships her vegetables and fruits? I think we have an example of it right here in the room.

PERRY: Tin cans.

TEACHER: Was tin mentioned among the minerals of California?

PERRY: No, Miss ———.

TEACHER: That's one thing that California would need. We shall have to see how much tin she has, and how much she needs to import from other states. You may look that up, Perry, when we go upstairs.

JULIA: In Florida they have most of the products they need. When we were studying Florida with the student-teacher, she told us that Florida depends upon us for her markets.

BARBARA: Lemons remind me of the citrus fruits they have in Florida. The limes taste so much like lemons.

TEACHER: Did you hear anything about limes, Barbara, in these reports? What other citrus fruits did we hear about?

CATHERINE: Oranges.

PAUL: Grapefruit.

TEACHER: Do you know where grapefruit comes from?

CATHERINE: Florida.

PERRY: Why is the fruit raised on the east side and not on the west side of the Sacramento Valley?

ANTHONY: The clouds couldn't pass over some of the mountains.

TEACHER: Will you hold that question for just a minute. We'll come back to that.

WILLIAM: How long is the Mohave Desert?

LUCY: It is 5,000 square miles.

TEACHER: You have given the area, not the length. Do you know the length, Lucy?

LUCY: No, Miss ———.

ANTHONY: Why is alfalfa grown so much in California?

TEACHER: It is a southern product. As we study Texas and other southern states, we shall learn that alfalfa is commonly raised as feed for cattle.

MURIEL: It grows best in warm climates as do the redwoods.

PERRY: Why don't the beans have to be irrigated?

ANTHONY: Why is the northern part different from the southern part of the state?

GEORGE: Could prunes sink a ship? (This remark was the result of reading a chart showing tons of prunes compared with ships of different sizes.)

NANCY: It is just that they grow so many of them.

TEACHER: What does this chart show us? (Points to chart on prunes.)

LOUISE: I was going to ask that question too.

MURIEL: How hot does it get in Death Valley?

TEACHER: Did you find the figures?

PERRY: 143 degrees, I think, in the shade.

TEACHER: It frequently is 120 degrees. That is very warm, isn't it?

DONALD: We haven't mentioned the north, we have mentioned the east and west. What grows on the north side?

TEACHER: The valley is so long we think of it usually as having just an east and west side. (Teacher draws a diagram on board to help explain this.) If we draw a line across it, the upper part would be north and the lower part south. I think we shall have to go on to the questions on the next report.

GEORGE: I saw a picture of a boat with scrap metal for Japan where it is made into toys and artillery.

WILLIAM: What is tungsten?

LUCY: It is used for making steel for fine tools and for electric lights.

TEACHER: Have you ever seen the inside of an electric light bulb? Those tiny filaments are made of tungsten.

GEORGE: I looked it up in the dictionary and it said it was a very fine metal.

TEACHER: The filament is even finer than a fiber.

BARBARA: Death Valley reminds me of the long strips of land in Florida, without any houses on them.

TEACHER: If you don't mind we shall go on to answer the questions about the variety of climate from north to south. This is a picture of the redwood trees that grow in the north. This is a tree from the south, although a cactus would be called a plant, not a tree. There is quite a contrast between a tree that would not fit into a schoolroom and the cactus plant.

ANTHONY: Climate and soil. It is a little bit cooler in the north because it is far from the equator. The climate is hotter in the southern part of California than in the northern part.

TEACHER: There is a big "if" to that remark. What would the "if" be? It is cooler in the north, and warmer in the south "if" or "unless" what?

DONALD: If the sun has direct rays.

PERRY: The northern part is cooled by the winds that blow across California.

TEACHER: Anthony's statement is true "unless" or "if" something. You have not answered the question.

JUDITH: If you are not too high up.

TEACHER: Yes, you must know both the latitude and the altitude. What is the latitude of California? Will somebody go to the map to find out.

BARBARA: (At map.) 41 or 42 degrees.

TEACHER: Where does it begin? About $32\frac{1}{2}$ degrees. From $32\frac{1}{2}$ to 42 degrees. That is the latitude. Now the altitude?

Teacher wrote on board—

    I Latitude $32\frac{1}{2}$ to 42 degrees

    II Altitude

ANTHONY: It has very high mountains and they are mostly all worn down. There are some young rugged ones. The eastern coast has the worn-down mountains.

TEACHER: We sometimes get mixed on east and west. You'd better go to the map and point to it.

ANTHONY: I mean the west.

TEACHER: Yes, the worn-down mountains are on the west. Where are the high rugged mountains?

ANTHONY: In the eastern part of the state.

TEACHER: What's the name of them?

GENERAL RESPONSE: Sierra Nevada.

NANCY: How high is Mt. Whitney?

ANTHONY: 510 feet.

TEACHER: It is over 14½ thousand feet high.

LOUISE: California has the highest mountains and the lowest land in the United States.

TEACHER: Lucy, you told us something very interesting about the lowest land in the United States.

LUCY: Death Valley is 276 feet below sea level so that an airplane flying in it can fly below sea level.

TEACHER: After gymnasium we shall go on and find out more about this. We still haven't answered the two very important questions you asked about the beans growing without irrigation when it does not rain, and about the products California needs from other states. Take your things and pass quickly to the door.

LESSON 6. ARITHMETIC

GRADE 4

Review of Zeros Involved in the Four
Fundamental Processes

TEACHER: Place arithmetic materials on your desks. We shall work with zeros this morning. Why are zeros sometimes troublesome? Can someone think of a reason? Do you think it might be because sometimes we forget what it says here? (Points to board.)

(On board.) Things to Remember About Zero.

1. Zero (0) means "not any" or "nothing."
2. 0 added to a number does not change the number.
3. 0 and a number equals the number added.
4. Zero times any number is zero (0).
5. Any number times zero equals zero (0).
6. Zero divided by any number equals zero (0).

What does that say, Sally? The first thing to remember?

SALLY: (Reads No. 1.)

TEACHER: That's a very important fact to have in mind about zeros. Let's just read through these other things to remember about zeros because I shall expect you to keep in mind these things while working with zeros.

MARIE: (Reads No. 2.)

TEACHER: We shall find an example of that as we do some of these problems.

ROGER: (Reads No. 3.)

EDWARD: (Reads No. 4.)

GEORGE: (Reads No. 5.)

DOROTHY: (Reads No. 6.)

TEACHER: Are there any questions about those things to remember? Let's begin with addition. All of these problems contain zeros in various positions. Will you begin, Emma?

EMMA: 7, 10, 14, 23, etc. (First addition problem.)

TEACHER: Will you add these columns, please?

(Teacher records figures as child gives answers.)

TEACHER: Which one of these statements would fit the figures in this column?

EMMA: (No. 3) o and a number, etc.

TEACHER: The next example, Ruth.

RUTH: (Reads second example while teacher records figures.)

TEACHER: You remember zero means "nothing" or "not anything." Zero and 2 is what? Then think of 10 and 2 is what? We have some examples this time that require a certain mark to make it complete.

PATRICK: The comma.

TEACHER: Yes, because it has something to do with hundreds and thousands. Where shall I put it?

TILLIE: Between 1 and 3.

TEACHER: The next example, William. You notice this time we start with zero. Keep in mind—zero and a number equals the number added.

WILLIAM: (Reads third example while teacher records figures.)

TEACHER: 11 and 7, think of 1 and 7. 18 and 4, think of 8 and 4. That's all, isn't it? Gustave, will you take the next one? I'll ask Henry to come to the board and take down the figures. (Gustave reads numbers from the board while Henry records them.)

TEACHER: Tell him, Janet. Let's all be ready; if a person hesitates we can all be ready to help him. Doesn't anyone disagree here?

TILLIE: 17.

TEACHER: Place the comma. What did you do when you came to zero?

GUSTAVE: Skipped right over it.

TEACHER: The next example. We are all thinking.

ROBERT: (Reads fourth example from board.)

TEACHER: 10 and 3, think of o and 3. You have one to carry. Where shall I put the comma?

ROBERT: Between the 7 and 3.

TEACHER: All of these examples so far have referred to which things to remember?

ROBERT: The first three.

TEACHER: The next one is dealing with United States money. Would the addition be any different, Dorothy? You don't add differently, but you do have something to remember. (Does example.) This would be a good place to put down the extra thing to remember. We must remember to keep the cent point in what position?

EMMA: One right under the other.

DOROTHY: (Goes on with example.)

GEORGE: 10.

TEACHER: George, will you help out here? Think of nothing and 9, then 10 and 9. Is there anything else to make that complete?

DOROTHY: $ sign.

TEACHER: How would you read that?

PUPIL: Six hundred sixty-nine dollars and ninety-eight cents.

TEACHER: Will you come to the board this time, Robert, and do the figuring? I'm going to ask Robert to do the work by himself.

ROBERT: (Does next example on board.)

TEACHER: Let's leave the addition for a few minutes. If there's time at the end of the period perhaps we shall complete these others. Let's think of subtraction, using zeros. Patrick, will you come to the board and work out the first example?

PATRICK: (At board, first subtraction example.)

TEACHER: You can fill that right in immediately, nothing and 6 is 6. In this next one, we have zero in a different position and more figures. Who would like to do this, Gladys?

GLADYS: (At board, second subtraction example.)

TEACHER: Are you going to place the comma? Does anybody disagree? You remain at the board and write down the figures for the next example. Raymond, will you do the thinking?

RAYMOND: (Reads answers to third subtraction example.)

TEACHER: Perhaps Raymond can't see; will you stand on this side, Gladys? Who hasn't had a turn and would like to try an example? Edward?

EDWARD: (Does fourth subtraction example.)

TEACHER: If we start with nothing, it will require what to make 8? You may use that way of subtracting and also get the correct answer if you do the work properly. Let's try one more with subtraction, using money. Helen, will you do the thinking?

HELEN: (Does fifth subtraction example.)

TEACHER: Shall I place the dollar sign? To check this work to be sure we have the right difference for any of these, what shall we do?

GEORGE: Add.

TEACHER: What would we add? What do we call the answer?

ROBERT: The difference.

TEACHER: Yes, difference or remainder. What do you call this part of the subtraction, the larger numbers?

PATRICK: Minuend.

TEACHER: Let's think about multiplication. Here we will find that there are other things to remember in the list. What should you do when a zero occurs at the end of a multiplier? What's the thing to do?

VIRGINIA: Put down the whole number.

MAY: Just put down the zero and multiply the rest.

TEACHER: As many as we find at the end of the multiplier.

MAY: (Reads first multiplication example.)

TEACHER: We must remember to place it at the end of the example. Will you do this example, May? Anyone, who has it right in mind?

MINETTE: 36.

TERRY: 68.

TEACHER: What would help May a little with this type of work?

RUTH: Study her tables.

TEACHER: Let's try another one. Where is the zero in this example? In what part of it?

RUTH: In between the end numbers in the multiplicand.

TEACHER: Would you show us how you work this out? I'd like everyone to observe. She said to put down the 6 and carry the 5, but if I see that the very next figure to multiply is a zero, I just put down the 5 because it would give us the same product. It saves time, doesn't it? Go on.

RUTH: Seven 4's are 28, etc.

TEACHER: Now we find that we have some zeros in addition. Is that correct, William?

WILLIAM: Yes, Miss ——.

TEACHER: Where shall I place the comma? Let's do this one next with the dollars and cents, Minette?

MINETTE: (At board. $6.73 x 108.)

TEACHER: Be ready to help boys and girls with any of these examples. I wonder if Minette will know what to do when zero occurs in the middle of the multiplier. Yes, put down the zero. Nothing times any number would be what? Always be zero. Do you think it would be necessary to write three zeros in the multiplier?

TERRY: Do not put down all the zeros.

TEACHER: Do we need three zeros here? What should we do?

EDWARD: We may multiply by one.

GUSTAVE: Go on with the next multiplier.

TEACHER: That's right.

ROBERT: (Adds the total in the example.)

TEACHER: I should like you to try one or two examples in division before we begin our individual work. Is there something wrong? I'm glad you noticed something, Emma.

EMMA: The dollar sign should be in the example.

TEACHER: Who will try the division where there are two zeros in the end of the dividend?

TILLIE: (Does first division example.)

TEACHER: What's one of the things to remember which fits this particular case?

TILLIE: Zero times any number is zero.

TEACHER: This is division, Tillie.

TERRY: Zero divided by any number equals zero.

TEACHER: We'll try one more. Let's try one where the zero comes in the middle rather than at the end.

WILLIAM: (Does next division example.)

TEACHER: Eight won't go into 2. Five 8's are what?

GUSTAVE: 40.

TEACHER: Who's ready? Nine 8's make what?

WILLIAM: 72.

TEACHER: How shall we write that remainder, as a fraction, over what?

WILLIAM: Put 4 over 8.

TEACHER: Can you think of ways in which work with zeros might come into our everyday lives?

TILLIE: My father gave me 50¢ for 5¢ boxes of ice cream to divide between 5 people.

TEACHER: Is this something that really happened to you?

TILLIE: Yes, Miss ——.

TEACHER: What do we need to know? Who would like to work this out? How much did Tillie spend for ice cream?

ROBERT: 25¢.

TEACHER: How much did Tillie say her father gave her?

ROBERT: 50¢.

TEACHER: Then what change did she receive?

ROBERT: 25¢.

TEACHER: Was there any work with zeros?

EDWARD: Yes, Miss ——.

MAY: I went to the store and bought some eggs for 35¢ and some bread for 6¢. My mother gave me a $1.00.

TEACHER: What did you have to do to know what to receive for change? Why am I putting this down as a column, Emma?

EMMA: You have to add.

MAY: Miss ——, that's all I got.

TEACHER: You would have to add to get the cost. How much would I get back? Do you want to do this yourself, or ask someone else?

MAY: Thomas.

TEACHER: You could really do this in your head. She wants to know how much change she will receive from one dollar.

THOMAS: Subtract.

TEACHER: Any zeros to come into this subtraction?

EMMA: Yes, Miss ——.

TEACHER: Let's remember to keep the cents placed in the cents column. What did you find to be the change?

GUSTAVE: 69¢.

TEACHER: Is that what you received for change, May?

MAY: Yes, Miss ——.

TEACHER: I have placed some pages for suggested practice on the board. This is work where you will have an opportunity to use your textbooks. I should like you to take one page for practice for each of the four processes with which we have been working. When your work is complete for all of these processes, I should like to have you pass your problems to me.

EMMA: How many of the pages shall we do?

TEACHER: Do just one page for each process. You may do more than one page if you wish but I think you will not have time to do more now.

RUTH: Do the numbers mean columns?

TEACHER: No, because in this case it doesn't happen to be placed in columns on the paper. Find the page and you will see what I mean. If you don't understand, show me the book and I'll help you.

MAY: May I do the problems here first?

TEACHER: If you do the whole page it will give you more practice.

TILLIE: What does the line between the numbers mean?

TEACHER: This hyphen means that you do the numbers from one through six.

TEACHER: Place the papers inside your books so that you may do the work upstairs. You may return quietly to your room.

. . . . .

Work with Zeros (on board)	Pages for Practice (textbook)	
Addition	Page 67	
	" 81	Rows 4, 5, 6
	" 256	Nos. 1-6
Subtraction	Page 83	Rows 3-6
	" 86	" 3 and 6
	" 294	" 1-5
Multiplication	Page 255	Rows 1-4
	" 268	" 3 and 6
	" 292	

LESSON 7. ENGLISH

GRADE 4

Measuring Pupils' Reading Comprehension

TEACHER: Open your books to test lesson 65. Take out the card and place it on the book. Close the book leaving your finger in the place. When I say "begin" open your books to test lesson 65, read the story through carefully and read the questions and answer as many of them as you can. If you do not know the answer to a question go back and read the story. Place the little squares in your card under test lesson 65 over the letters which belong to the correct answer. The letter which belongs with a word is always before it, rather than after it. Only one letter in a square. Do not erase and do not mark over. You will have three minutes in which to do this work. Begin!

(Children at work on test while teacher times them.)

Test Lesson 65—

One day I saw a kingbird sitting on a fence post near my garden. Suddenly, he flew down to some pea vines that were climbing up some cords stretched between posts. Several times he fluttered up above the posts and then dropped down again. Wondering what could be the matter I hurried down the path, but the bird flew back to the fence before I reached the vines. Hanging from the end post was a piece of cord about a foot long. It was the end of one of the rows of cords on which the vines were climbing. The bird had been trying to get this for his nest. I went back to the house for a pair of scissors and cut the cord, letting it fall to the ground. Then I left the garden. I had hardly reached the house again when the bird flew down and picked up the cord. Then he flew up to a hickory tree in which he was building a nest.

1. The kingbird was sitting on a (a) gate; (b) post; (c) tree; (d) house.

2. The fence was near a (a) house; (b) tree; (c) garden; (d) street.

3. The vines were climbing on (a) wires; (b) posts; (c) cords; (d) fences.

4. The bird was trying to get a piece of (a) cord; (b) wire; (c) vine; (d) straw.

5. I went to the house for a (a) a pair of scissors; (b) piece of cord; (c) pair of gloves; (d) piece of bread.

6. I left the cord on the (a) post; (b) fence; (c) ground; (d) tree.

7. When I went to the garden the bird (a) hurried down the path; (b) hid in the vine; (c) flew to the fence; (d) flew to his nest.

8. While I was in the garden the bird was probably (a) singing; (b) watching me; (c) eating; (d) picking the cord.

9. When I left the garden the bird (a) flew away; (b) got the cord; (c) followed me, (d) got a worm.

TEACHER: Stop! Keep your pencils. The answer to the first one, Mildred?

MILDRED: The kingbird was sitting on a post (b).

TEACHER: If you had the wrong answer cross it off by drawing diagonal lines from opposite corners of the square. Number two, Lilly?

LILLY: The fence was near a garden (c).

TEACHER: Number 3?

BARBARA: The vines were climbing cords (c).

TEACHER: You left out one word. Read that again please.

BARBARA: The vines were climbing on cords (c).

TEACHER: Number 4?

CARL: The bird was trying to get a piece of cord (a).

TEACHER: Number 5?

ROBERT: I went to the house for a pair of scissors (a).

TEACHER: Number 6, John?

JOHN: I left the cord on the ground (c).

TEACHER: Number 7, William?

WILLIAM: When I went to the garden the bird flew to the fence (c).

TEACHER: Number 8, Clarice?

CLARICE: While I was in the garden the bird was probably watching me (b).

TEACHER: Number 9, Margaret?

MARGARET: When I left the garden the bird got the cord (b).

TEACHER: Just to be sure, I'll check: 1-b, 2-c, 3-c, 4-a, 5-a, 6-c, 7-c, 8-b, 9-b. All those having nine correct stand. Now you're sure you have them down just right. What shall I put in the grade score?

HARRIET: 8.2.

TEACHER: What does that mean?

HARRIET: A child has the reading ability of a pupil in the eighth grade second month.

TEACHER: Is there anyone who didn't get any of them answered correctly? One answered correctly? Two answered correctly? 3? 4? 5? (Joseph, stands.) Joseph, what do you put in your grade score?

JOSEPH: 5.3.

TEACHER: What does that mean?

JOSEPH: That the child has a reading ability of a pupil in the fifth grade three months.

TEACHER: Are you above grade, below grade, or just up to grade?

JOSEPH: Above grade.

TEACHER: Six correct? What is your grade score?

NICKY: 5.7.

TEACHER: Are you above grade or below grade?

NICKY: Above grade.

TEACHER: Seven right? What is your grade score?

SALVATORE: 6.5.

TEACHER: What does that mean?

SALVATORE: It means that a child has the reading ability of a pupil in the sixth grade five months.

TEACHER: Are you above grade or just up to grade?

SALVATORE: Above grade.

TEACHER: Eight correct? What is your grade score?

MILDRED: 7.2.

TEACHER: What do you rank, Mildred?

MILDRED: Above grade.

TEACHER: All children above grade, stand. (Whole class stands.) Very good. Be seated. Alice may read the paragraph orally. Come up to the front.

ALICE: One day I saw a kingbird sitting on a fence, etc. to completion.

TEACHER: Alice, where was the kingbird sitting?

ALICE: On a fence post.

TEACHER: I'd like to have the sentence read that tells the answer to the second question.

ROBERT: One day I saw a kingbird sitting on a fence post near my garden.

TEACHER: The sentence that answers the third question?

OLGA: Suddenly he flew down to some pea vines that were climbing up some cords stretched between posts.

TEACHER: The sentence that tells the answer to the seventh?

ELIZARETH: The bird was trying to get a piece of cord.

TEACHER: Read the question first and then the sentence which tells the answer.

ELIZABETH: When I went to the garden the bird flew to the fence.

TEACHER: You read the sentence that tells the answer. Who can do it?

EDWARD: When I went to the garden the bird flew to the fence. Wondering what could be the matter I hurried down the path, but the bird flew back to the fence before I could reach the vines.

TEACHER: I'd like someone to read the fifth question and then the answer.

MARGARET: I went back to the house for a pair of scissors and cut the cord, letting it fall to the ground.

TEACHER: The sentence that tells the answer to number eight?

SARAH: While I was in the garden the bird was probably watching me.

TEACHER: Who can do it?

ROBERT: I had hardly reached the house again when the bird flew down and picked up the cord.

TEACHER: What was the question?

ROBERT: While I was in the garden the bird was probably watching me.

TEACHER: Place your cards in the books and close the books.

LESSON 8. SOCIAL STUDIES

GRADE 6

Concept of How Geography of British Isles Affects Their World Relations

TEACHER: Gertrude is the chairman for today.

GERTRUDE: We have been working on the unit, the British Isles, in our geography, and this morning we are ready to give reports. The problem that we are concerned with is how the geography of the British Isles has helped Great Britain to take a leading place in the civilized world. The first report is about "Climate" and is given by Florence.

FLORENCE: The British Isles have a stimulating climate good for physical and mental work. The British Isles are situated between 50 and 55 degrees north latitude and are in the path of westerly winds in June which is summer, and January which is winter. Let us compare the climate of London with that of New York. New York is farther south than London, therefore we would expect New York to have cooler summers and warmer winters. I shall draw an illustration proving that it hasn't. (On board draws maps of British Isles and United States, indicating by crosses the positions of New York and London.) This is London and this is New York.

TEACHER: Just what is it you are trying to show?

FLORENCE: That New York is farther south than London. It is also in the path of the westerly winds and it would seem that New York would have a cooler summer and warmer winter than London and we are going to prove that it hasn't. The winds blowing from the ocean are westerly winds and temper the cold of winter as well as the heat of summer.

TEACHER: Let's be sure that we have this straight. What kinds of winds are they?

FLORENCE: Westerly winds.

TEACHER: They are blowing across the United States but they are blowing across what kind of area?

FLORENCE: Land area.

TEACHER: Whereas, the British Isles winds blow from where?

FLORENCE: The ocean.

TEACHER: What difference does that make?

FLORENCE: The winds blowing from the ocean temper the climate.

TEACHER: In cities on the Atlantic seaboard the winds that come in across the land are warm, while in the British Isles the winds come directly from the ocean.

FLORENCE: I have here a map showing the isotherm readings. In the British Isles the temperature in winter is 40 degrees and in summer 56 degrees. (On board 56—40 is 16.) The range of temperature is 16 degrees and we know that is a low range. From this map we can see that on the western part of the British Isles there is more rainfall than on the eastern part. The mountains block the rainfall before it all can reach the eastern part.

TEACHER: We can probably tell from that report the surface of the land.

FLORENCE: There are lowlands in the eastern part of the British Isles. Are there any questions?

FLORA: There might not be sufficient rainfall for all kinds of agriculture.

TEACHER: You didn't tell us how many inches of rainfall are represented by the dark blue.

FLORENCE: Eighty inches.

TEACHER: There are not many regions where there are eighty inches of rainfall.

FLORENCE: (Pointing to map.) There are 40″ and 60″ right around here and 20″ and 40″ over here.

TEACHER: What conclusion would you make from those numbers? I think Flora started to make that conclusion. Those figures don't mean very much to us. You may forget the numbers.

FLORA: There is always enough rainfall for some kind of agriculture.

DAVID: That range is called the middle range.

FLORA: The rainfall is well distributed in the British Isles.

TEACHER: That is another good idea to keep in mind. What is the problem we have under consideration this morning? You may not remember it just as we have it in our notes.

WILLIAM: How the geography of the British Isles has helped Great Britain to take a leading place in the civilized world.

TEACHER: How has climate helped the British Isles to take a foremost place in the world? We have this big problem and the first topic is climate.

EDNA: It is a stimulating climate. This helps the people to be energetic and intelligent and when they have these qualities they will help the country.

TEACHER: In what way will they help commerce?

GRACE: In a stimulating climate they can work with their brains as well as their hands in both winter and summer.

TEACHER: We might change that a little bit—say it better.

RICHARD: It is a climate that is good for using your heads as well as your hands.

SUSAN: A stimulating climate is a climate that is good for mental and physical work.

TEACHER: Good. The next report.

GERTRUDE: Ellen will tell about the "Variety of Surface Features."

ELLEN: There is a variety of surface features in the British Isles. There is no land that goes below sea level. The highest mountains are the ones in northern and central Scotland. The highest peak is Ben Nevis which is 4000 feet. There are mountains in Wales called the Cambrians. These are low and rugged. The Scottish Highlands are high granite peaks. The cliffs drop from 3000 to 2000 feet. The Pennines are in the northern part of England. Pennines are low rugged mountains sometimes covered with heather. Southern peninsula England is a moor. There are a great many bogs in Ireland and they are made up of peat so that no pasture lands or farms may be made on this. Peat is used for fuel to heat the farm houses. Are there any questions or additions?

WILLIAM: What is a moor?

ELLEN: It is a low land sometimes covered with heather.

FLORA: What color on the map shows the highest mountains?

ELLEN: You can't see it very well but it is a light yellow. Light green is 1000' to 2000', dark green is 300' to 500'.

WALTER: The highest peak is only 4000'.

JEAN: What is heather?

ELLEN: It is a kind of vegetation.

TEACHER: And has a very pretty blue flower. As you make a mental picture of a map of the British Isles, what are you going to picture? What do you think about the surface of the British Isles?

MAY: Mostly highlands.

TEACHER: What is the dominant color on that map?

MARY: Green.

ELLEN: Dark green is 300 to 500 feet.

TEACHER: There are no very high mountains and yet there is no land that goes below sea level. Have you something else?

ELLEN: This has nothing to do with my report but I want to tell you about the prime meridian. Time is measured from this meridian which runs through Greenwich. Every 15 degrees, as you go west to east, you take off an hour. Longitude is measured east and west around the earth. Any questions or additions?

FLORA: Do you know if we were going from America to Europe how many hours we would have to go back in Europe?

TEACHER: You may know that from listening to the radio broadcasts. How many hours would you take off?

RICHARD: 5 hours.

TEACHER: How does surface help the British Isles to take a foremost place in the world?

ISABEL: There is access to the sea.

TEACHER: What does that mean?

ISABEL: It is near the sea.

TEACHER: It is surrounded by water and has excellent harbors.

WALTER: They couldn't be attacked by other nations. They are well protected.

GERTRUDE: The next topic is "Variety of Names." Mary will report for this group.

MARY: In connection with the British Isles there are many different names. I will tell you what each name stands for.

British Isles—are two large islands.

United Kingdom—is the official name of northern Ireland and Great Britain.

Great Britain—England, Scotland and Wales.

England—is the largest part of Great Britain.

Scotland—is the northern part of Great Britain.

Wales—is the western part of Great Britain.

Ireland—is made up of two divisions, northern Ireland and Irish Free State.

Irish Free State—part of the British Empire but not of the United Kingdom.

Are there any comments or additions?

WALTER: How many divisions are the British Isles made up of?

MARY: Two islands, Great Britain and Ireland.

TEACHER: It would appear that there are more than two divisions.

MATTHEW: Five.

TEACHER: How many really are there?

WILLIAM: Two.

GERTRUDE: "Invasions of Several Peoples" will be given by Michael.

TEACHER: We are talking about how people have helped the British Isles to take a foremost place in the world.

MICHAEL: The present day people are intelligent, energetic, skillful and inventive. The invading peoples of the British Isles were the Celts, Romans, Angles, Saxons, Danes and Normans. The Celts possessed the land for centuries. They made use of the tin of Cornwall in their own industries and as a means of attracting traders from afar. Julius Caesar took Roman legions to Great Britain. For 500 years the Romans lived and built there. After they withdrew, other invaders came from other countries and entered Great Britain. They pushed the Celts into the mountainous regions of Northern Scotland, Wales and western Ireland. The Anglo-Saxons came from what is now Germany, and Danes from the Scandinavian peninsula. Later Normans came across the English channel from France. Marriages took place among the invading races and among the people they conquered. The English of our time are descendants of mixed races. Some of England's greatness is due to the qualities of all these people.

FLORA: A lot of the things we use today were invented by English people. James Watt, a Scotchman, invented the modern steam engine, and it was George Stephenson, an Englishman, who built the first locomotive. There is no question about the reliability and skill of the British workmen.

TEACHER: What is the origin of the people living in the British Isles? Who are some of their ancestors?

ANN: Celts.

DAVID: Normans.

PETER: King George VI can trace his ancestry back to William the Conqueror, a Norman.

TEACHER: Good. You have been reading the newspaper. We will not have time for another report. Notice the many interesting maps. The pupils that made them might go up and show us what the maps illustrate.

GLORIA: This is a map of natural products in the British Isles. Birmingham—iron ore, Sheffield—steel, Belfast and Dundee—linen, and Manchester—cotton.

WALTER: Fishing is my map topic. Most of the fishing is done in the North Sea. Aberdeen and Hull are great fishing ports. Herring and mackerel are caught.

JOHN: This map shows the coal fields in Glasgow. Here are the Newcastle field, South Wales field, Northumberland field.

TEACHER: There is an interesting saying in connection with coal in Newcastle. When one says something that is unnecessary, one says "That's like carrying coals to Newcastle." Why?

PETER: They don't have to carry it because the coal fields are already there.

LESSON 9. ARITHMETIC

GRADE 5

Practice in Solving Problems Related to Pupils' Interests

TEACHER: I would like to have all the children except those in the sporting problem group go quietly to the blackboard or work in their places as they have planned. The sporting group may open their books [87 : 1937] to their first problem. Who would like to do it?

ARTHUR: James is thinking about buying a bicycle that costs $22.75. If he takes the money for that from the $49.79 in his bank account, how much will he have left? Subtract $22.75 from $49.79.

TEACHER: The problem asked "How much will he have left?"

ARTHUR: He will have $27.04 left.

TEACHER: Ready with the next No. 5.

JOSEPH: After he buys his bicycle, will he have enough money left to buy a $45.00 radio? He hasn't enough money.

TEACHER: The next question?

JOSEPH: If he has more than enough tell how much he will have left after he bought the radio. Subtract $45 from $27.04.

TEACHER: But you just told me he hasn't enough. Why do you suppose that is put in there?

JOSEPH: Just to fool you.

TEACHER: Yes. Let's go on with the next part.

JOSEPH: $27.04 from $45, he needs $17.96.

TEACHER: Page 33.

ANTHONY: Ted bought an old bicycle for $10.00. He spent $2.50 to have it repaired. Then he sold it for $14.00. How much did he gain on it?

TEACHER: What was the cost?

ANTHONY: $12.50.

TEACHER: Are you telling how much it cost?

ANTHONY: $10.

TEACHER: (Pointing to $12.50.) What does this represent?

ANTHONY: The total cost. Place the $ sign, point off two places from the right.

TEACHER: What do we call the $14?

ANTHONY: Selling price.

TEACHER: How do we always find the gain in examples of this kind?

PERRY: Subtract the cost from the selling price.

TEACHER: The next problem. Who's ready?

SAMUEL: My brother can ride 10 miles an hour on his bicycle. How long will it take him to go 25 miles? Divide 10 miles into 25 miles.

TEACHER: Why do we divide?

SAMUEL: To see how long it will take him.

TEACHER: You are right, but we should know why we do it.

ANTHONY: To find how many hours it takes him.

PERRY: To find how many 10 miles there are in 25.

TEACHER: Yes, to find how many 10-mile stretches there are. What do you get?

SAMUEL: (Teacher wrote down figures on the board as Samuel did problem.) Two and one-half—so it will take two and one-half hours.

TEACHER: Page 15. Stephen.

STEPHEN: Our automobile registered 209 miles on Monday. On Thursday it registered 2708 miles. The car had run between how many miles since Monday?

TEACHER: You read your first figure wrong. Look at this figure. (On board.) 2009. Stephen—two thousand nine. You might place the comma there to help you read the number. What's the other number? Read that.

STEPHEN: Two thousand seven hundred eight miles.

TEACHER: All right, what do we do with these figures?

STEPHEN: Subtract.

TEACHER: Why?

STEPHEN: Because you want to find out how many miles the car traveled since Monday. 699 miles.

TEACHER: You must find the difference between the two numbers. The sixth example on the same page.

PERRY: A man bought a $750 automobile and paid $425.50 on it. How much did he still owe? We subtract $425.50 from $750.

TEACHER: Why?

PERRY: To find out how much he still owes.

TEACHER: How could you check that to be sure that it is correct?

JOSEPH: By adding.

PERRY: (Reads example from board as teacher writes figures.)

TEACHER: If this number is like this number it is correct. What shall we use for the answer?

PERRY: Still owed.

TEACHER: We haven't heard from you, Jerome.

JEROME: Mr. Jones bought an automobile for $750. He spent $284.49 for repairs and then sold it for $1200. How much did he gain on it?

TEACHER: What problem is this like?

JEROME: The third one on page 33.

TEACHER: Yes, like the bicycle one. (Jerome does problem with teacher at the board.) What does this represent?

JEROME: How much it cost the man. Then he sold it for $1200. Subtract $1034.49 from $1200.

TEACHER: Read your answer, please.

JEROME: $165.51 gain.

TEACHER: This group may go quietly to work now, and the next group turn to page 15. Who's ready?

MURIEL: At the rate of six apples for 25c how much will a dozen apples cost? 6 apples are a half dozen, multiply by two. 50c.

TEACHER: Yes, twice as many apples will cost twice as much money.

JULIA: Ted bought a dozen oranges at 40c and sold them for 5c each. How much did he make on them?

TEACHER: This is another find-the-gain problem. What did Ted have to find in order to find the gain?

JULIA: Selling price and cost.

TEACHER: How much would he sell each orange for? How much did he sell a dozen oranges for?

JULIA: 5c, 60c. You subtract 40c from 60c. 20c was the gain.

TEACHER: Page 19. Catherine, are you ready?

CATHERINE: (Read problems.) Nine oranges cost 54c. One orange costs 1/9 of 54c or 6c.

TEACHER: That was an easy one, wasn't it? Page 24. This is the page that Irene and Lucy have just done at the board, so we shall omit that just now. Let's turn to page 33.

NANCY: Oranges are selling two for 5c. How much will a dozen cost?

TEACHER: How many 2's are there in twelve?

NANCY: There are six, and six times 5 is 30c. That makes 30c the cost per dozen.

TEACHER: Six times as many oranges would cost six times what?

NANCY: Six times as much money.

TEACHER: Page 37.

FAY: If you sell 6 eggs at 3¢ apiece, you will get 18¢. If you spend the 18c for 2c stamps you will get nine stamps.

TEACHER: How do you know?

FAY: You divide two into 18.

TEACHER: The fourth one.

LUCY: We have three eggs for breakfast every morning. How long will a dozen eggs last us? (Does problem.) Four mornings.

TEACHER: How could Lucy have done that another way?

NANCY: If one dozen eggs lasts four mornings, you may say that two dozen eggs would last eight mornings, because twice as many eggs will last twice as long.

TEACHER: Yes, two dozen is twice one dozen. Now you may go quietly to your work. Irene has not done a problem for us.

IRENE: When oranges are selling two for 5c what will 6 oranges cost?

TEACHER: Then you want to find out how many groups of two oranges there are in six. Six is how many times two?

IRENE: 3. Three times as many oranges will cost three times as much money. 15c.

TEACHER: Right. This group ready. The 3rd problem.

DONALD: Tom went to a boy's camp this summer for two weeks. He had to pay $10 a week for board; his carfare cost him $2.47 each way;

and he spent $2.50 besides. Can you find how much his camping trip cost?

TEACHER: There are one or two catch words in this problem. What is one word you must see if you are going to work the problem correctly?

JACK: Each way.

ANTHONY: $10 each week for board and he stays two weeks.

TEACHER: Yes.

DONALD: If he stayed two weeks it would cost him $20 for board and $4.74 for carfare.

TEACHER: You have made a mistake on the carfare. How much was it for one way?

DONALD: $2.47.

TEACHER: For both ways?

DONALD: $2.47 x 2 is $4.94. Point off two places.

(On board.) $20.00
4.94
2.50
———
$27.44

TEACHER: Will you girls in the back please tell us what you did?

LOUISE: We subtracted the number left from the number received and then put the number down here.

TEACHER: What was the problem, Louise?

LOUISE: It is a florist problem. A boy takes care of a flower shop and he had to fill in a chart when he gets through.

TEACHER: It is really a stock-taking problem.

LOUISE: There were 15 pots of tulips received and 4 pots of tulips left, then you subtract 4 from 15 to see how many were sold. There were 11 sold. Then we multiplied the cost which is 90c a pot. 11 x 90c gave us $9.90. The total which he had amounted to $88.55.

TEACHER: Did you get the right answer the first time?

LOUISE: Yes, Miss———.

TEACHER: Antone, can you tell us about your problem?

ANTONE: You have to find out how many yards it is from the tent to the other places in the camp. We had to measure from his tent to the dining room. On this diagram it is 8″. 8″ at 40 yds. to an inch is 320 yards.

TEACHER: Tell us about one that you did, Jack. 6″ on your rule represents how many yards?

JACK: 6 times 40 yards, 240 yards.

TEACHER: Perry, are you ready with your problem? Tell us just what you started to do. I know you haven't had time to finish it.

PERRY: The first problem is to find how many feet it is from Home Plate to First Base.

TEACHER: Some of us may not be familiar with baseball. Show us what you drew.

PERRY: Our scale is 1 inch equals four feet. This measures 21" by 4' — 84'. It should be 90' from Home Plate to first base. I got 90' when I did it before.

TEACHER: Yes it should be 90'. Your diagram isn't accurate. It is a good thing to check it to see. Try it again upstairs. How many people have finished the set of problems they were supposed to do? (Pupils who have finished stand.) Take your things and pass quietly to the door.

LESSON *10. ENGLISH*

GRADE *4*

Use of Dramatization to Promote Desirable Skills and Habits for Speaker and for Audience *

TEACHER: Are we all ready for the plays? Before we have the plays presented, let us have some reminders for speakers as well as for members of the audience. What should speakers remember when presenting plays?

ROBERT: Talk loudly.

TEACHER: Any other reminders?

RUTH: Speak distinctly.

TEACHER: What should members of the audience remember?

GLADYS: Sit well.

MAY: Not to talk to your neighbor, nor to think out loud.

WILLIAM: Keep quiet so as not to distract characters.

TEACHER: May we have the play which you will announce first, James?

JAMES: (James announces the title of the play, *The Beginning of Negro Slavery* and presents the characters by introducing the pupils who take the various parts. These pupils include Patrick, William, George, Raymond, Terry, and Gustave. As stage manager he mentions briefly the scene of the play and with which characters the play opens. The foregoing pupils present the play which is not printed here. At the close James asks for comments and class discussion continues.)

JAMES: Any questions about the play?

TEACHER: Any comments from members of the audience? Did you enjoy it Helen?

HELEN: Yes, Miss ——.

* The two plays dramatized in this lesson are by Tucker and Ryan [91 : 1927].

TEACHER: Is there any way the people in the play could improve it if they give it again? (Pause.) I would suggest that the characters speak a little more slowly. It would be better. I should like to ask a question of the captain. Why did you call attention to the Negro's big chest and muscles?

TERRY: It showed he was ready for work.

TEACHER: Did you want to show his strength?

TERRY: Yes, Miss ——.

TEACHER: That was the idea. Robert and Edward may get the properties ready for the next play. Emma, you announce the play.

EMMA: (This play, *Cherry Pie,* is introduced and presented in a similar manner to the first play. Pupils portraying characters in the play are Edward, Pearl, Roger, Ruth, Robert, Emma, and Tillie. Following the presentation of the play, classroom discussion continues.)

TEACHER: Members of the audience, is there anything you wish to say? Is there any way the people in the play could improve it if it were to be presented again?

MAY: Walter and Roger shouldn't have gone in front of Emma.

TEACHER: What should they have done?

MAY: They should have gone in back of Emma.

RAYMOND: Ruth should have gone to the fire to pick up her pie.

RUTH: I didn't realize the pie was on the fire.

TEACHER: Isn't that where the pie should be for baking?

ROBERT: I was going to say the same thing that Raymond said.

TEACHER: There is one thing that I should like to speak to you about. How many enjoy reading historical stories? (All stand.) Then everyone does. Has anyone read any books that are listed on the board? Which one have you read, Robert?

ROBERT: *American History Story Book* [86:1912].

TEACHER: Which one have you read, May?

MAY: *Stories of Early American History* [88:1913].

TEACHER: Where did you obtain that?

MAY: I obtained it from the library.

TEACHER: You will notice that I have included play-books as well. Perhaps a group would like to select a play for an auditorium program next Tuesday.

APPENDIX C

General Matters Pertaining to Observation

I. Observer's first and last name: ....
....
Normal School or place located: ....
....
Business address (city and state) ....
....
Type of position held ....

II. Rank with figures 1, 2, and 3 the most prevalent observation tech-
nique used by teachers-in-training (students) when observing classes
in your normal school or locality:
........Use running notes
........Use a seating-chart and code
........Use no recording device until after the lesson
........Specify any other technique here: ....
....

III. Do observation guide sheets of any type usually accompany the observation of classes by those students? .... Rank with figures
1, 2, and 3 the most prevalent type:
........A statement of the past work of the class.
........A statement of the major objective of the lesson to be observed.
........A statement indicating what to look for during the observation.
........Specify any other here: ....
....

IV. Regarding your observation of a classroom lesson:
Underline which of the following techniques you used: made full
running notes; used a code on a seating-chart (code as mimeo-
graphed for purpose); no recording until after the lesson.
State grade observed ....
State subject observed ....
State school where observed ....
State number of pupils in the class observed ....

V. Regarding your checking the choices of statements in the accompanying form, called "Check List for Observing Pupil Activity in the Classroom":

The spaces between the multiple-choice items in the check list are left for your rephrasing of the descriptions wherever you think changes should be made or considered. Your suggestions and criticisms will be of considerable value when a revision of the items is made and your co-operation in this matter will be fully appreciated.